DEATH NOTICES

IN

The South-Carolina Gazette

1732-1775

Compiled and Edited by
A. S. SALLEY, JR.

Death Notices
In The South Carolina Gazette, 1766-1774

BY MABEL L. WEBBER

From the files in the library of the Charleston Library Society,
CHARLESTON, S. C.

CLEARFIELD

Death Notices in The South-Carolina Gazette 1732–1775
Originally published
Columbia, South Carolina, 1917

Death Notices in The South-Carolina Gazette 1766–1774
Originally published
Columbia, South Carolina, 1933

Reprinted for
Clearfield Company, Inc. by
Genealogical Publishing Co., Inc.
Baltimore, Maryland
1996, 2001

International Standard Book Number: 0-8063-4656-6
Made in the United States of America

PREFACE

In 1917 the Historical Commission of South Carolina (now the South Carolina Archives Department) published a volume that was intended to include all of the death notices appearing between the years 1732 and 1775 in the Charleston Library Society's file of *The South Carolina Gazette*. The copy had been carefully prepared by Mr. A. S. Salley, then Secretary of the Commission; but unfortunately that part of it which contained the notices taken from the issues between September 15, 1766, and January 2, 1775, was lost by the printer and, for this reason, omitted from the published volume. It was not until sixteen years later that the missing notices were printed. As compiled at that time by the late Miss Mabel L. Webber, they were published in four installments (pages 55-61, 88-95, 149-56, and 211-17) in Volume XXXIV of the *South Carolina Historical and Genealogical Magazine*, of which Miss Webber was then serving as editor.

The Archives Department has been generously granted permission to include the Webber compilation in this second printing of the original edition of the *Death Notices*. In order that copies may be made available at a moderate price the two parts have been reproduced by the lithoprint process, and the dimensions of the page have been slightly reduced. The part prepared by Mr. Salley has not been altered in any way; that prepared by Miss Webber has been changed only to the extent of eliminating running heads and renumbering the pages. The latter change has simplified the preparation of the index which it was thought should be added to this part. The index was made by Wylma Wates, Editorial Assistant in the Archives Department.

J. H. Easterby
Director

CONTENTS

DEATH NOTICES

IN

The South-Carolina Gazette

1732-1775

———————

Compiled and Edited by
A. S. SALLEY, Jr.
Secretary of the Historical Commission of South Carolina

———————

From the files in the library of the Charleston Library Society,
Charleston, S. C.

———————

Printed for
THE HISTORICAL COMMISSION OF SOUTH CAROLINA
By The State Company, Columbia, S. C.
1917

INTRODUCTION.

The first issue of *The South-Carolina Gazette* appeared on Saturday, January 8, 1732, and it was published continuously once a week until December, 1775, when it temporarily suspended publication on account of war conditions. It resumed publication on Monday, April 14, 1777, with its name changed to *The Gazette of the State of South-Carolina*, and continued to be published, under various changes of name, until some time during the year 1802, when it finally passed out of existence.

The death notices here given are from the files from the beginning of the paper to its first suspension and change of name.

On Tuesday last died Joseph Haynes, which was the 17th Day after his being first taken ill of the Small-pox, of which Distemper (agreeable to our last) he was, the Day before his Death, in a fair Way of Recovery, and supposed to be out of Danger, but upon shifting himself took cold, which occasion'd so sudden and fatal an Alteration. We hear the Nurse who attended him in his Illness, is ordered to continue in the House where he died for 20 Days, by Way of Quarentine.

On Wednesday last died of a Flux, at Mr. Stephen Beaton's in this Town, one Mr. Tho. Cole, a Person who came from Providence to this Place about 6 Months ago for his Health. A few Days before his Death, he made his Will, and left the Chief of his Effects to his Brother in England, and of his Will made the said Mr. Beaton Executor, who, having since his Death open'd his Boxes, before proper Witnesses, found therein 727 Onnces of Silver, and about the Value of 50l. Sterling in Gold, besides several Parcels of small Goods, as Thread, Tape, &c. in which he had been a Dealer. He was a Dissenter, and a Man of fair Character. (Saturday, April 1, 1732.)

On Monday last, after a very long Disorder, died, Mrs. Mazyck, the Wife of Mr. Isaac Mazyck, sen. Merchant of this Town, in an advanced Age, and on Wednesday following she was interr'd in the Church-Yard of this Place, in a very handsome Manner, being attended to her Funeral by most of the chief Merchants, and publick Officers of the Province, that were then in Town. (Saturday, April 8. 1732.)

On Monday Morning last died Mr. *William Hammerton*, Naval Officer of this Port. (Saturday, April 29, 1732.)

The same Day* one ——— *Thomas*, belonging to the Indian Trade, died suddenly at the Bowling Green House, as he was going to take Horse, being in all Appearance in perfect Health just before. (Saturday, July 1, 1732.)

On Sunday last, at the Seat of the Hon. Col. *Broughton*, President of his Majesty's Council for this Province, died Madam *Johnson*, his Excellency the Governor's *Lady*; after a pretty long Indisposition. She was a Lady so remarkable for the good Qualities of a Wife and Mother, that his Excellency's Loss can be supported only by that happy and steady Disposition of Mind *He himself* is Master of. By all her other amiable Qualities, in Life, she had gained the universal Esteem of this *Province*, and consequently her Death proves a General Concern; which was in some Measure testified by the Number of Persons, of all Ranks, that paid their last Respects at her Funeral, which Ceremony was performed in the Church at *Charlestown*, in the most handsome Manner that possibly it could. We hear that most People design, on this Occasion, to put themselves in Mourning. (Saturday, July 8, 1732.)

On Monday Morning last died Mr. *Eleazer Philips*, Printer in this Town. As did the next Day Mr. *Brawn* the Dancing Master, at a Gentleman's Plantation in the Country, and both after a very short Illness. Some others in Town, have died suddenly of Fevers lately. (Saturday, July 15, 1732.)

On the 24th of last Month, was drown'd in crossing over a Creek near Cape Roman, Mr. John Bampfield, our Provost Marshal, with one Mr. Westlead, and 4 Negroes, by the oversetting of their Canoe.

On Sunday last was drown'd, Mr. Morris Harvey, the Pilot, by the oversetting of the Canoe, as he was going ashore on Suillivan's Island. And

On Tuesday last died Mr. William Johnson, his Excellency the Governor's second son.

Yesterday Morning died Mr. Henry Hargrave, Deputy Secretary of this Province. (Saturday, August 5, 1732.)

We hear from *Providence*, that his Excellency *Woods Rogers*, Esq, Governor of that Place, died there the 20th of last Month. (Saturday, August 12, 1732.)

---

*Wednesday.

One Day last Week, one Richard Birmingham, belonging to his Majesty's Ship the Shoreham, was drowned in Wappoo Creek, over against Col. Lucas's Plantation, by oversetting of the Canoe, in endeavouring to get the Grappling up. (Saturday, October 7, 1732.)

On Thursday last, one Thomas Morrison, being disordered in his Senses, drowned himself: And the next Day the Body was taken up, and the Coroner's Inquest sat on the same, and brought in their Verdict *Non compos Mentis.* (Saturday, October 14, 1732.)

Died suddenly of an Apoplexy, on Monday last, within sight of his Plantation at Goose-Creek, *Mr. Jacob Satur*, a wealthy Merchant of this Town. (Saturday, December 9, 1732.)

On Friday the 23d of this Instant, died *John Herbert*, Esq; sole Commissioner of the *Indian* Trade, at his Plantation on *Goose-Creek*, a Gentleman very much esteemed for his many good Qualities, especially his strict Justice and Impartiality in the Execution of his Office. His Death is lamented by all who knew him. (Saturday, March 31, 1733.)

On Monday last, died the Lady of the Honourable Col. Broughton, President of his Majesty's Council of this Province, a Lady of great Piety and Charity, and very much lamented, by all that knew her. (Saturday, June 30, 1733.)

Last Week, one *James Ballenis*, an *Indian* Trader, coming from *Savannah* Town, drop'd from his Horse and died suddenly. (Saturday, August 25, 1733.)

On the 23d last past in the morning, one *Martin Dunn*, belonging to his Majesty's Ship the *Alborough*, happened to be with *Benjamin Story* in his Periauger in the Northern Branch of *Stono River*, and striking at an Alligator, fell over board and down to the Ground immediately: No doubt but the Alligator made a good breakfast on him. (Saturday, March 2, 1734.)

We are informed that Capt. MCcliss, loaden with Pitch and Tarr and bound from this Port to London, after having been a Fortnight at Sea, had the Misfortune that his Vessel sprung a leak and sunk, and that he and two of his Men narrowly escaped by putting out the Yawl: A Brigg being then in sight, and seeing them in Distress, came up and took them on board, but after having been in her about two Weeks, Capt. MCcliss and his two Men, and the Capt. of the Brigg with two of his Sailors were all at once washed over board. (Saturday, March 9, 1734.)

On Monday last died here, after a few Days Illness, *George Head*, a Gentleman who came here with a Cargo from *Phila-*

delphia and *Providence* in the Schooner *Jolly Batchelor*, and
was decently buried the same day on the Friends Burying-
Ground. (Saturday, July 6, 1734.)
On Tuesday the 13th Instant died near Ashley River in the 104th
Year of her Age, Mrs. Elizabeth Baker, her Maiden Name was
Elizabeth Wilson, she was born in Wiltshire, in a Town called
Shruton the 18 of August 1630, she lived in England 27 years, in
Barbados 23 years, and in Carolina 54 years: She had 12
Children, 2 of them being alive yet, 25 Grand Children, and 43
Great Grand-Children, and the same Day she died, one of her
Great Grand-Daughters, the Spouse of Coll. Palmer, was deliv-
ered of a Child.

On the 14th died the Reverend Mr. John Witherspoon, a Pres-
byterian Minister at James's Island. (Saturday, August 17,
1734.)
On Friday the 16th Instant in the night died suddenly *Roger
Lownds* Esq; who a Week before was appointed Lieutenant of
his Majesty's Snow the *Happy*.
Sunday last died Doct. *Thomas Cooper*, a Man of good Character, and very much regretted. And yesterday died Mrs. Baker,
Spouse of Mr. *John Baker*, an eminent Merchant in this Town.
Wednesday last came into this Harbour the Sloop *Lydia*, bound
from Philadelphia to *Georgia;* They came to Anchor off the Barr
on the 19th in the evening, and the next morning in weighing
the Anchor one of the Handspikes broke, and gave the Mate of
the said Sloop, *Benjamin Newble*, such a blow on the right side
of his head, that he fell down and soon after expired, which
occasioned the Loss of their Anchor. (Saturday, August 24,
1734.)
On Sunday last died Mr. John Franklin, a Gentleman of a very
good Behaviour, which made him esteem'd and beloved by every
body, and as he died Batchelor, we hear he is very much
regretted by a young Lady with whom he was going to be married, if Death had not taken him away. (Saturday, October 12,
1734.)
On Saturday last between twelve and one o'Clock died, after a
long and lingering Sickness, His Excellency Robert Johnson
Esq; Captain General, Governor and Commander in Chief in
and over this his Majesty's Province, and was decently interred
on Monday last in a Vault near the Altar in Charles-Town
Church. His Pall was supported by the Gentlemen of the Council, and his Corps was attended to the Grave by the Lower House

of Assembly, headed by their Speaker, and a numerous Body of
Gentlemen and Ladies who came from all Parts of the Province,
where timely Notice could be had of his death, to pay their last
Respects to one whom they might justly look upon as their
common Father. The Troop and the two Compagnies of Charles-
Town Foot appeared on this melancholy Occasion, to add to the
Solemnity of the Procession. The principal Mourners were his
Excellency's two Sons and two Daughters, his Brother in Law
Thomas Broughton Esq; our present Governor, and his Family.
His Excellency died in the 59th Year of his Age, and in the 5th
of his Government. He had on his Advancement disposed of all
his Patrimony in England, so that his Interest might concur with
his Inclinations in promoting the Welfare of that Country his
Majesty had done him the Honour to intrust him with the Care
of, and accordingly always kept up a good Correspondence with
the Assembly, as they were all fully convinced by the whole
Tenor of his Conduct, that the Interest of the Province. lay
principally at his Heart. But it will be needless to enlarge upon
a Life & Character so well known, and which have render'd his
Death so universally and deservedly lamented over the whole
Province. (Saturday, May 10, 1735.)

On Fryday the 16th Instant about twelve of the Clock, died the
Wife of the Hon. PAUL JENYS Esq; Speaker of the Hon. the
Commons House of Assembly. (Saturday, May 24, 1735.)

On Monday night last Capt. *Robert Robinson*, Master of the
Billander, called the *Oliver*, got up, and was seen by one of the
Passengers, going forward to the head of the Vessel, and no
•further notice taken of him, but in the morning was miss'd,
supposed to be fallen over board. A Sloop coming up the River
last Friday saw the Sharks tosting up a Man in the Water, and
tearing him to Pieces, having on a Scotch Plad Banyan, confirms
this supposition, he having been that night in such a dress. (Saturday, August 9, 1735.)

On Saturday last died here Capt. *Anthony Mathews*, an eminent
Merchant & Settler of this Province, who by his Industry, Fru-
gality & Improvement in Mercontil Affairs, acquired one of the
greatest Estates in this Country. He first arrived in this Province about the Year 1680. Now near 55 Years since, and died
lamented in the 73d Year of his age, and was decently burried
on Monday last. But what is observable is, that his *Pall* was
supported by six of the ancient Inhabitants of this Town, hardly
one of whom had seen less than 40 Years revolve since their first

Arrival in this Province, and whose several Ages put together amounted to about 400 Years. A sufficient proof, this, that Carolina *is not* one of the *most unhealthy* Climates on Earth. (Saturday, August 30, 1735.)

On Thursday last at Christ-Church Parish died the Reverend Mr. *Fullerton*, late Minister of the said Parish, and was decently buried the Fryday following. (Saturday, September 6, 1735.)

The same Day (Saturday before) died Mr. *Andrew Allen* an eminent Merchant in this Town, and was decently buried on Monday last. (Saturday, September 13, 1735.)

On Wednesday the first of *October* died Mrs. *Dowding*, spouse to Mr. *Joseph Dowding* of *St. James Goose-Creek* Shop keeper, she was a Patron of true Vertue to all that knew her, and as she liv'd so she died a good Christian. (Saturday, October 11, 1735.)

On Thursday last died after having been delivered of a dead Child, Mrs. *Guichard*, Spouse to the Rev. Mr *Guichard*, Minister of the French Church in this Town. (Saturday, January 24, 1736.)

On Wednesday last died *Alex: Parris* Esq; (after an Indisposition of *Six* Weeks) at the Age of *Seventy-four*, wanting a few Days, one of the oldest Settlers in this Province, in which he has been *Forty-five* Years; He had been *Forty-one* Years married to his Wife, who died nigh *Two* Years past, and from her had 53 Children and Grand-Children, who are sensible of their Loss, as he had always shown himself with the Affection of a loving Husband and a tender Parent. He had the Honour to be in all publick Offices in this Government, Civil and Military, both of Honour and Profit, in all which he never had regard to his private Interest. He had very much at Heart the building and finishing the present Church in *Charles-Town*, and was not wanting either by Persuasion or Example to do all that in him lay to compleat the same: He always shew'd himself to be a humane and charitable Benefactor to the Poor, and of a generous and benevolent Disposition to all his Friends and Mankind in general. At his own request his Corps was interred on Friday Evening in a decent plain manner, attended by most of the Inhabitants of this Place.

And Yesterday Mr. Isaac Mazyck sen. departed this Life, aged 77 Years. (Saturday, March 13, 1736.)

On Thursday morning died after a lingering Sickness, Mr. *Joseph Massey* of this Town Gunsmith, he was Captain of one of the Foot Companies, and was the first that engraved and printed the Paper Currency of this Province, a Man universally beloved and esteemed for his Ingenuity, mildness of Temper and prudent Conduct. (Saturday, May 15, 1736.)

From *Savannah* in *Georgia* we hear, that on the 2d of *April* last died at *Bathurst Bluff* in the 57 Year of her Age the Lady of Sir *Francis Bathurst*, with an Inflammation in her side, she was brought to *Savannah* the next day, and interred, Gentlemen and Ladies of the best rank in this Place, also the King *Tomochichi* with his Queen attending her Corps. Her death is much regretted, having always been a loving Wife, an affectionate Mother, and a true Housekeeper. (Ibid.)

On Friday the 14th Instant Mr. *William Moore* being with some other Gentlemen hunting, one of them firing at the Deer, miss'd and shot him through the Body, whereof he soon died. (Saturday, May 29, 1736.)

On Monday last died at his Plantation near Charlestown *Charles Hart* Esq; who had been Secretary of this Province during the Administration of several Governors, and which Office he resign'd a few Years ago, and spent the rest of his Days to an advanced Age in a single State at his Plantation; his Corps was brought to Town on Tuesday morning and decently buried that Evening.

As was likewise *Sam: Jones* Esq; one of the Representatives in the General Assembly for the Parish of St. Paul's in Colleton County, who died the same Day. And

On Thursday following died after a short Indisposition Mr. *John Baker*, an eminent Merchant of this Town, and Copartner with *Paul Jenys* Esq; He was a Gentleman of good Sense, and a polite and engaging Conversation; generous and obliging to his Friends, courteous and affable to all, and plain and sincere in his Dealings; so that he justly gain'd the Love and Esteem of all that knew him, and his Death is much lamented by his intimate Friends and Acquaintance He was decently interr'd last night, and his Funeral attended by a great Number of Persons of all Ranks, under the firing of Minute Guns from most Vessels in the Harbour. (Saturday, August 28, 1736.)

Yesterday morning died after a few Days illness, *Rowland Vaughan Esq*; Attorney at Law. (Saturday, September 4, 1736.)

On Friday last week died on *Daniel's* Island, Mr. *Is: Lessene*, in the 62d Year of his Age, and on Saturday following *Elias Horry* Esq; aged 72 Years, one of the eldest Settlers in this Province, and who by his merits and Services to the Country, has left behind him a very good Character, he died in this Town, and was decently burried on Sunday in the French burrying Ground. (Saturday, October 2, 1736.)

On Monday last the Wife of Mr. *Brian* a Carpenter, coming home by herself in the Evening, she went into the Kitchin, and sitting before the Fire she fell into a Fit, (as 'tis supposed, she being frequently seized with Fits) and tumbling with the Chair on her Back in the Fire, no body then being present, she was found burnt to death in a miserable manner. (Saturday, January 1, 1737.)

On Thursday last died after a long and lingering Sickness Mr. *Isaac Chardon* an eminent Merchant of this Town, whose Death is very much regretted, and yesterday his Corps was carried over to *James Island* to be interred there. (Saturday, January 15, 1737.)

A very melancholy Accident happened this Week, Capt. *Bellinger* at *Ashley* Ferry sending one of his Sons with a Negro in a Canoe to Town, in order to return to the boarding School, they both were missed, and great Search being made after them, they were found dead on Tuesday last sticking in the Mud in the said River, their Arms clasping one another. (Saturday, January 22, 1737.)

On Tuesday Morning died Doct. *Turner* of this Town, having been the Day before visiting his Patients; he had made his Will two Days before, wherein he bequeathed all his Estate to Mrs. *Hannah Booth* (who had been his Housekeeper) for her Lifetime, and then to gó to the Poor. (Saturday, July 2, 1737.)

Yesterday departed this Life after a long and tedious Sickness, Mrs. *Garden*, Spouse to the Rev. Mr. *Garden*, Minister of this Town: Her Removal is a sore Loss to an afflicted Husband and four small Children she left behind her; she is to be interr'd this Day. (Ibid.)

On Wednesday last departed this Life at his Plantation on *John's* Island *Paul Jenys* Esq; an eminent Merchant of this Town, and one of the greatest Dealers in the Province, his great Abilities caused him to be chosen Speaker of the Honble. the House of Commons of the late Assembly, of which Station and Trust he acquitted himself with great Applause of all his Friends, by whom he is very much regretted. (Saturday, July 23, 1737.)

On Sunday last died *Daniel Green* Esq; one of his Majesty's Justices of the Peace for *Berkley* County and a great Trader in this Province, he was interred the Day following, and his

Funeral attended by a great Number of People of all Ranks.
(Saturday, August 13, 1737.)
Early this Morning died Mr. *Sam. Eveleigh*, an eminent Mer-
chant of this Place, after a tedious Indisposition, in the 66th
Year of his Age: He had been a Resident here near 40 Years,
was ever a hearty Friend to the Province, and a remarkable
Promoter of Trade; he was justly esteemed for the Lenity and
Uprightness of his Dealings and his extensive Benevolence to
Mankind. (Thursday, March 30, 1738.)
Landgrave *Thomas Smith* departed this Life on Tuesday last in
the 75th Year of his Age, having been 54 Years in this Province.
(Thursday, May 11, 1738.)
On Tuesday last Mr. *James Kinloch*, eldest Son of the Hon *Jas:
Kinloch* Esq; one of his Maj Hon. Council of this Province, died
at his Father's House at *Santee*, of a violent Fever and Impos-
thume in his Head, after an Illness of 12 Days. He arrived in
this Province about 15 Months ago, having been 5 Years in
several Parts of *Europe* for his Education and Improvement.
As the many good Qualities this young Gentleman (only 20
Years of Age) was indow'd with, made him justly esteemed by
all those who had the Pleasure of his Acquaintance, so his Death
is now greatly lamented by his unconsolable Parents, Relations
& others who knew him. (Thursday, August 31, 1738.)
On Sunday the 17th Inst. died at his Plantation in *Goose-Creek*,
Mr. *William MacKenzie* late of *Charlestown* Merchant, after 5
Days Illness of a Fever, aged 45 Years. He came into this
Province about 22 Years ago, and has since carried on a con-
siderable Trade in *Charlestown*, 'till lately (having acquired, by
his honest Industry a competent Estate) he gave off his Business
in Trade, and retired to said Plantation in the Country.
A Gentleman whose Character needs no Embellishment in this
Place; but whose happy Conduct of Life, in all Paths of Religion
and Virtue, has imprinted it fair and amiable in the Minds, and
easy on the Tongues of all that knew him. Nor Envy nor ill
Nature dares venture to detract from or gainsay his exemplary
Piety; rare Temperence and Purity; his Integrity, flowing
Benevolence and diffusive Charity; his House open to the
Stranger, his Hand to the poor and needy, his Compassion and
Assistance to all that were desolate or oppressed: In Sum, that
he was a pious, sober, honest, peaceable, good natured, charitable
Man; in one Word, a sound and sincere *Christian*. No one, in

his Sphere, more generally beloved! Nor any one's Death more generally lamented!

And suitable to his worthy Conduct of Life, was his peaceful End. He beheld the *King of Terrors* approaching him, with the greatest Firmness and Composure of Soul, and often repeating,— *let me die the Death of the Righteous, and let my End be like his,* he calmly resigned it into the Hands of his Creator and Merciful Saviour, and fell asleep.

His Corps was brought to Charlestown, to the House of Mr. *Ja. Crokatt,* from whence it was conveyed the Monday Evening following to the Place of Interrment, attended by his mournful Widow and Daughter, and all the Inhabitants of any Note that were then in Town. (Thursday, September 28, 1738.)

This Day died *Mrs. Elizabeth Izard* Wife of *Mr. Joseph Izard;* she was in the 19th Year of her Age, and had been married just 4 Months: Her Death is much lamented by all her Relatives and Acquaintances, on account of her singular Sweetness of Temper, and many other good and amiable Qualities. (Thursday, January 25, 1739.)

On Monday last departed this Life the Lady of the Honourable *William Bull* Esq; President and Commander in Chief in and over this Province; and was interred on Thursday last in very handsome Manner, the Funeral being attended by the Council and Assembly, with several other Officers and Gentleman of Distinction. (Saturday, March 24, 1739.)

By Letters from *Cape-Fear* we are informed of the Death of *Thomas Clifford* Esq; at that Place; he was a Gentleman, who to much good Sense had joined a competent Share of Learning; in Conversation was entertaining and facetious, in Life extremely inoffensive had a hearty Benevolence to all Mankind, and just Sentiments of Liberty and Happiness. (Saturday, August 25, 1739.)

On the 18th Instant, died Gilbert Higginson *Esq; Surveyor of his Majesty's Customs for this Province and the* Bahama-*Islands.* (Saturday, October 27, 1739.)

"The Reader is desired to read in Gaz. No. 296, Gilbert Higginson Esq; Surveyor and Comptroller, Comptroller having been left out."—Saturday, November 17, 1739.

On the Twelfth of last Month, died the Honourable Robert Wright Esq; late Chief Justice of this Province, and the Court of General Sessions being to sit within a few Days after, his Honour the Lieutenant Governor was pleased to grant a special

Commission to Thomas Dale Esq; one of the Assistant Judges, to hold the Court of General Sessions, Pro hac Vice, as a sufficient Number of the Members of his Majesty's Council, could not on Account of the late Sickness, be then assembled on the Seventh Day of this Instant his Majesty's Council met, and his Honour the Lieutenant Governor, with their Advice, appointed Benjamin Whitaker Esq; Chief Justice of this Province, who on the next Day received his Commission, and took the several Oaths appointed by by Law to qualify himself for the Execution of the said Office. (Saturday, November 24, 1739.)

On the Twenty-first of *January* last, died *Nicholas Trott* Esq; Doctor of Laws, who for several Years past was Chief Justice of this Province, during the Time the Government was in the Hands of the Lords Proprietors, and at several Times had Commission from the Admiralty of *England*, to be Judge of the Court of Vice-Admiralty here. And continued in the Office of Chief Justice, till the Lords Proprietors were ousted of the Government. After that he lived private and retir'd from all publick Business, and applied himself wholy to perfect his designed Explication of the Original *Hebrew* Text of the new Testament; and finish'd one large Vol. in Folio fit for the Press some short Time before his Death. He was born *January* 19, 1662-3, and died *January* the 21st, 1739-40, being 77 Years of Age. (Saturday, February 2, 1740.)

We hear from *Maryland*, that the Hon. Coll. *Alex. Spotswood* died there on the 5th of last Month. (Tuesday, July 1, 1740.)

Last Sabbath Morning died *here*, and was decently interr'd the Day following, amidst all the Sable Expressions of Grief, Mr. Charles Peronneau, *Merchant*, in the 28th Year of his Age.— *A Name* that will always be mention'd with Honour by all who have felt the Influence of his Acquaintance—He was a dutiful *Son*, a loving *Brother*, a sincere and steady *Friend*, and indeed an Ornament to his *Country;* which has produced but *few* of his *Equals*, and *ought* to be thus publickly acquainted with the Loss it sustains by his Death.—By a laudable Industry, and quick Capacity for Business, under the smiles of Providence, he had amass'd a considerable Interest, and laid a probable Foundation for all the little Happiness *this* World can promise; but was not so immers'd in *Business*, as to forget the Improvements of a *Genius*, for which *Nature* had distinguish'd him:—No; instead of prostituting his *Leisure-Hours* to the common Vices and vain Amusements of *Youth*, he devoted them to *reading*, and had collected and perused many Writers of the *first* Class and Character—He had a good Taste in *Poetry*, and had well digested several excellent *Pieces*, as well *Theological* as *Philosophical*— As he had a Thirst for *Learning* in all it's most valuable Branches; so with a just Balance, and due Mixture of *Judgment* and *Imagination*, he became a great Master of his *Pen;* which he discover'd in several occasional *Letters* to his intimate Friends, of that *Spirit*, *Elegance* and *Correctness*, that they might bear the *Examination* of the *severest Criticks* of the Age, and could not fail of the *Applause* of all *candid* Judges: And if he arriv'd to this Perfection in Writing by the mere Force of *his own Powers* and Application, what might we not have expected from him, had he stood nearer the *Fountains* of Science, convers'd more freely with *Academics*, and dwelt among the *Muses*—Nor had he less of the *Gentleman* than of the *Scholar*; for he understood all the Forms of *Civility*, the Rules and Decencies of *Conversation;* and how to indulge an innocent Freedom, without any Breach or Inroad upon Religion and Modesty.—To sum up his Character, he was of an admirable *natural* Temper, of much *social* Virtue, and more than a Tincture of *serious Religion;* which he was of too catholick a Spirit, and had too much Grandeur of Soul to confine to *a Party*, or Points of *more Indifference.*—A Man of such Merit, and so many natural and moral Accomplishments, snatch'd away in his *Prime* and Flower, is no *private* Loss; but a monitory and affecting Instance of the 'Vanity of *Human Life;* while his *Character* deserves Immortality, and survives for the Imitation of *young Gentlemen*, who, with him, would live *beloved* and die *lamented;* without which, the most pompous *Funeral-Procession* is but the *Burial of an Ass.* (Thursday, October 23, 1740.)

On *Tuesday* last about 5 in the Afternoon, one *Gideon Norton*, a Ship-Carpenter in *Tradd-street*, having cleaned his Gun, loaded it at the Desire of his Wife, then brought it in to shew her how clean he had made it, and the Muzzle being towards her, it unfortunately went off, and shot her in the right Breast through her Body, whereby she instantly died. The next Day the Coroner's Inquest having viewed the Body, and examined several Witnesses, it appeared, that the said *Norton* and his Wife had lived together in mutual Love from the Day of their Marriage till this sad Accident, whereby the disconsolate Husband lost one of the best of Wives, having left behind several young

Children. The Jury brought in their Verdict *Casual Death.* (Thursday, November 27, 1740.)

On *Saturday* last died here Mr. *Peter Fillieux,* aged 86 Years: He was one of the first Settlers in this Province, having lived in it 55 Years: He was under the sensible Decays of Nature for several Years past, and may be truly said to have died of that incurable Distemper Old Age. (Thursday, January 29, 1741.)

On the 29th of *December* last, died Mrs. *Desire Peronneau,* Wife of Mr. *Alexander Peronneau* of this Town, aged 59 Years. (Ibid).

On the 10th Instant, died Mrs. *Isabel Kimberly* of this Town, Widow, aged 73 Years. (Ibid.)

And on the 14th, died Mrs. *Mary Smith* also of this Town Widow, aged 66 Years. (Ibid.)

On the 22d Day of *March* last, departed this Life Mr. *Henry Wood,* in the 68th Year of his Age; he was the third Child born in this Province, and is an Instance how illgrounded are the Prejudices some Persons entertain against this Climate, as if few or none arrived at any remarkable Age, whereas for the Number of Inhabitants, there are as many Persons advanced in Years in this Colony as in most other Places: It is indeed granted, that the Youthful and the Vigorous are more liable to be cut off by Fevers, &c. in the warmer Regions, than in such as are colder; but then it must likewise be granted on the other Hand, that, as Wine is reckoned to be Old-Mens Milk, so those Persons, who by Temperance and a good Constitution escape thro' Youth and Manhood, generally enjoy a good Old Age, being cherished by that kindly Warmth which is so agreeable to their Natures. As a Proof of this many Persons might be mentioned, particularly Mrs. *Baker,* who died in the 104th Year of her Age, Mr. *Underwood* in his 100th; Mr. *Simmonds* in his 80th; and Mr. *Wm. Elliott* in his 78th, besides several others, who have been inserted in this Gazette a few Months past. (Thursday, April 2, 1741.)

On Saturday last died at his Plantation, in the 39th Year of his Age, very much lamented by all his Neighbours and Acquaintances; *William Fuller,* Esq; Major of the first Troop of Horse in this Province, and the next Day was decently interred. (Thursday, April 30, 1741.)

Last Saturday arrived here, from *Barbados,* Mr. *Gabriel Escott,* Merchant, in a very languishing Condition, and expired suddenly Sunday Afternoon, about the 42d Year of his Age. He was a Man of strict Honesty, and so much Good Nature, that his Death is greatly regretted by as many as had the happiness of being intimately acquainted with him. He was decently interr'd Monday Evening. (Thursday, May 7, 1741.)

On Sunday last died much lamented by all who knew him, Mr. *William Wallace*, an eminent Merchant of this Town, and the next Day was decently interred. (Thursday, June 4, 1741.)

We hear from *Georgia*, that Capt. *Richard Nortury* was lately kill'd in a Duel with Capt. Desbrisay. (Ibid.)

On Saturday last died Mrs. Susannah Brewton, Wife to Coll. Miles Brewton, much lamented by all her Acquaintance; She was about Seventy Years old, Six and Thirty of which she spent in this Province. (Thursday, July 30, 1741.)

On Sunday last died much lamented, Capt. *Thomas Gadsden*, who has been Collector of his Majesty's Customs in this Province for about 19 Years past. (Saturday, August 22, 1741.)

By a Letter from *North Carolina*, dated the 17th of *August* last, we hear * * * * That *Samuel Woodward*, Esq; Collector of that Place, lately died there, and that 'twas remarkable, Four Collectors have died there in less than *Seven Years*. (Saturday, September 19, 1741.)

April 20th died, much lamented by all who had the Pleasure of her Acquaintance, Mrs. HANNAH DART, Wife of *John Dart*, Esq; the many amiable and excellent Endowments of Mind she possessed, her singular unaffected Piety, Virtue and Goodness, rendered her an Ornament to her Sex, and are so well known, that as they stand in no of, neither can they be rendered more conspicuous by any Thing that can here be said: These made her Friendship highly desirable while living, and her Name honourable and precious, now gone. (Postscript to Saturday, May 1, 1742.)

Saturday departed this Life, after a tedious Indisposition, Capt. *Bruce*, late Commander of the *Hawk* aforesaid, much lamented by all his Acquaintance. (Monday, June 14, 1742.)

On Wednesday last died Mr. HENRY SELWIN, Merchant, much lamented by all who had the Pleasure of his Acquaintance. His mild and generous Temper, his affable and courteous Behaviour secured him, while in Life, a general Esteem. He was carefully observant of religious Duties, and contemned those Vices too prevalent amongst us, and, tho' but early in Days, was possessed of a competent Knowledge of useful Literature: The next Day he was interred, in a Manner suitable to his Degree and Character. (Monday, September 27, 1742.)

The same Day died Mr. *Paul Douxsaint*, much respected while
in Life, and now and as much lamented, as he had ever distinguished himself the most affectionate Husband, indulgent
Parent, kindest Master, and the sincerest Friend. (Ibid.)
From *Ponpon*, we hear, That *John Cook*, Esq; lately died there.
And, from St. *John's* Parish, we have News also of the Death of
Andrew Broughton, Esq; (one of the Brothers of our late Lieutenant Governor.) Two Gentlemen whose shining Qualities
are too well known in this Province, to require any Account of
them herein. (Monday, November 15, 1742.)
On the 1st Instant departed this Life, aged 76 Years, Mr. *Henry
Peronneau*, sen. He has lived almost 56 Years in this Province,
in which Time he has acquired a large Fortune, with a fair Character. (Monday, June 6, 1743.)
On Sunday last dyed the Spouse of *Henry Izard*, Esq; one of
the Daughters of the late Governor *Johnson*.
We hear that Mr *Thomas Jones*, of *Ashley River*, was drowned
last Week as he was fishing. (Monday, June 13, 1743.)
In a letter, dated "Charles Town, June 18th, 1743", to "Mr.
Timothy", of *The South-Carolina Gazette*, Hugh Anderson gave
a full account of the life and character of William Stirling,
"younger Son to Sir *William Stirling*", who died in Charles
Town on that day. (Monday, June 27, 1743.)
The same day [Friday], in a sudden Squall of Wind, a Boat in
the River overset and sunk; one of the Men in her (Mr. *Wm.
Dandridge*) was drowned.
John Johnston, well known in this Town, was likewise drowned
the same Day, near *Sullivant's* Island. (Monday, July 11, 1743.)
From *Virginia* we hear, that on the 18th of *April* last died there,
in the 88th Year of his Age, the Hon. and Reverend Mr. JAMES
BLAIR, Commissary of that Colony; President of the College of
William and Mary; Rector of Bruton Parish, and one of his
Majesty's Honourable Council in Virginia; and some Time Pres-
ident of that Colony. (Monday, July 25, 1743.)
And on Friday died Capt. *Edward Palmer*, Commander of the
Snow *Florinella*, lately arrived from *Piscataqua*. (Monday,
August 15, 1743.)
Major *John Porter*, a very considerable Dealer at *Brunswick*,
died there about the 20th of July last. (Ibid.)
Yesterday died Capt. *George Bowler*, Commander of the Ship
George & Henry, which lately put into this Port from *Jamaica*.
(Monday, November 21, 1743.)

On Monday last died after a tedious Indisposition, Mrs. Pinckney, late Wife of the Hon. Charles Pinckney, Esq; one of the Members of his Majesty's Council; and on Thursday she was interred in a handsome Manner, the Funeral being attended by His Excellency the Governor, both Houses of Assembly, and other Persons of Distinction. (Monday, January 30, 1744.)

On Thursday we had a violent Storm of Lightning, Thunder and Rain, here.—The Lightning has done considerable Damage to *St. Philip's* Church, the Steeple, and Organ, and killed Mr. *Anth. Furnis* who was work in the said Church, hanging one of the Bells. (Monday, April 30, 1744.)

On Saturday last died much lamented, Mr. *John Gwynn*, of this Town Merchant, and last Night he was decently interred. (Monday, September, 24, 1744.)

Friday was sev'n night, about One in the Morning expired in his Sleep, Colonel Miles Brewton, Powder-Receiver of this Province, and in the 70th Year of his Age. What is very remarkable, it was just that Day 61 Years, since He and his Two surviving Sisters first accompanied their Parents into this Country. This Instance joined to many others, that might be produced of ancient Settlers (some few of whom were prior, and several much later) might be urged as a prétty strong Argument to remove a too common though mistaken Prejudice, entertained by our Northern Neighbours against Us, as if we were a Colony of Youths, and that Grey-Hairs would not flourish in this Climate; whereas, it might be easily demonstrated, as well from Principles of Reason, as from Experiences, that in Proportion to the exact Number of Inhabitants, the Balance of aged Persons would turn out in our Favour. But this by the Way; As it is undoubtedly the Duty of every rational and accountable Being earnestly to endeavour like the Good Old-Man deceased to persevere in a constant and uniform Course of Vertue; so every Man, who from a well ordered Conversation here, has formed any pleasing hope, that his Peace and Happiness are seated above, would, I believe, ardently desire, like Him also, to vanish from the Earth, and to find such an easy and placid Passage into a glorious Immortality.

Swift was his Flight, and short his Road,
He *clos'd* his Eyes, and *saw* his God.—

Last Wednesday died also, Mr. James Matthewes, worth a very considerable Fortune; a Gentleman much esteem'd in his Life, and whose Death is generally regretted. (Monday, July 22, 1745.)

On Tuesday last departed this Life, Mrs. *Pringle*, the Wife of *Robert Pringle*, and Mrs. Eveleigh, the Wife of *Samuel Eveleigh*, Esq; two ladies of the most distinguishable Qualities, and unaffected Goodness, they were universally esteemed, and now lamented by all who had the Pleasure of their Acquaintance. (Monday, June 9, 1746.)

Yesterday died suddenly, Capt. *John James*, Master of the Snow *Eveleigh*. (Monday, July 29, 1746.)

On Saturday last died, *Alexander Murray*, Esq; of the Naval Office, a Gentleman of an universal good Charactér. (Saturday, October 4, 1746.)

A few Days ago died here in a very advanced Age, Mr. *Richard Grimstone*. We shall give our Readers some better Account of this Gentleman in our next, if it can be got. (Monday, January 19, 1747.)

The same Day [Saturday before] died, in the 33d Year of her Age, Mrs. *Lucretia Moultrie*, the Wife of Mr. *John Moultrie* an eminent Physician in this Town, a Gentlewoman possessed of every Quality that could render her an Ornament to her Sex. (Monday, May 11, 1747.)

On Sunday the 31st ult. died the Rev. Mr. *Robert Betham*, Assistant to the Rev. Mr. Commissary *Garden*, Rector of this Parish. He was of *Queen's*-College in *Oxford*, and some Time Curate of *Ware* in *Hertfordshire;* a sound Divine, and a good Preacher; which join'd with an exemplary good Life and Conversation, rendered him much beloved and esteemed in this Place, and agreeably whose Death is no less lamented. (Monday, June 8, 1747.)

The same Night [Friday before] died, Mr. *William Saxby*, Searcher for this Port. (Ibid.)

Last Saturday departed this Life, in the 27th Year of his Age, the Rev. Mr. *Thomas Kennedy*, Minister of the *Scots* Meeting-house in this Town. AMASIUS (to whom we are very much obliged) has in the following Lines, given us so just a Character of that Gentleman, that it is needless to say any more here, than that we wish his Example were follow'd. (Monday, August 31, 1747.)

A few Days ago, died, much lamented, after a lingering Indisposition, and in the 45th Year of her Age, the Lady of the Hon. *Benjamin Whitaker*, Esq; our Chief Justice. (Wednesday, January 6, 1748.)

This Morning died in the 45th Year of his Age, the Rev. Mr. *Daniel Dwight*, Rector of *St. John's* Parish in *Berkley* County. (Monday, March 28, 1748.)

On Sunday the 24th Instant departed this Life, *Benjamin Godin*, Esq; formerly an eminent Merchant of this Place, but of late Years, (after having acquired a plentiful Estate) had retired from Business, and lived for the most part at his Country-Seat in *Goose-Creek*. A Gentleman of unblemished Character for Integrity, Benevolence, and every Moral Virtue. A good Neighbour, A sincere Friend, A kind and indulgent Husband, A tender Parent, and a valuable Member of this Community. (April 27, 1748.)

Mr. *Thomas Hallum* is appointed (by Capt. *Hamer*) Commander of His Majesty's Ship the *Glasgow*, in the Room of Capt. *Lloy'd* who died here on the 21st ult. (Monday, October 3, 1748.)

This Day died, Mr. *Hugh Anderson*, Master of the Free-School near this Town. (Monday, November 21, 1748.)

On Wednesday last died Mr. *Kenneth Michie*, and about 10 days before him, Mr. *Benjamin Michie*, his Brother and Co partner, both eminent Merchants of this Town. (Monday, November 6, 1749.)

On Friday Night died much lamented, Capt. *James Taite*, late Master of the *Charming Judith*. (Monday, November 13, 1749.)

Yesterday Morning died, universally lamented, in the 51st Year of his Age, Mr. BENJAMIN SAVAGE: A Gentleman many Years eminent in the Mercantile Way, (by which he had acquired a large Fortune with Honour and Reputation) and valuable for the many good Qualities that rendered him beloved by all who had the Pleasure of his Acquaintance. (Monday, July 23, 1750.)

There lately died, at his Plantation in *St. John's* Parish, the Hon. *John Colleton*, Esq; one of the Members of his Majesty's Council. (Monday, August 13, 1750.)

This Morning died suddenly, Capt. *Henry Keller*, Commander of his Majesty's Ship *Mermaid* lately arrived from *England;* he was reputed a good Officer, and much beloved by the People he commanded. (Monday, September 10, 1750.)

Yesterday Afternoon died, aged 50 Years, THOMAS DALE, Esq; esteem'd a Man of great Virtues, Abilities and Learning in general, and in his Profession of Physic in particular, in which he took his Doctors Degrees at *Leyden* in the Year 1724 or 25: In his public Character (for he has been a Judge in the supreme Courts of this Province about 16 Years past) he always acted with great Integrity and Honour; and in his private Life exhibited a truly amiable Character, being possessed of many Virtues and Qualifications which made him valuable and agreeable to his Friends and Acquaintance, and without Envy, Malice or Resentment to his Enemies, for such he, like many other good Men, undeservedly had: He was open, generous and free in his Sentiments; and from his great and extensive Reading had a great Fund to entertain in Conversation: He was a loving, tender and affectionate Husband, a kind Neighbour, a humane Master, and a sincere and hearty Friend, a Lover of true Religion, and a Practiser of the Rules and Precepts of it; and has died as sincerely lamented, by all who had the Happiness of an intimate Acquaintance with him, as any Man ever did. (Monday, September 17, 1750.)

Last Friday Night died, *Samuel Wragg*, Esq; an eminent Merchant, possessed of a very large Fortune. (Monday, December 3, 1750.)

Yesterday departed this Life, aged 62 Years, very much lamented, particularly by his Parishioners, and by every one who had the Pleasure of an Acquaintance with him, the Rev. Mr. *William Guy*, Rector of *St. Andrew's* Parish for upwards of 30 Years past: Of whom it may be truly said, *He lived the Life of the Just, and died the Death of the Righteous.* (Monday, December 10, 1750.)

On tuesday last died greatly lamented JOHN RUTLEDGE, Esq; (brother to the Hon. *Andrew Rutledge*, Esq; speaker of the Commons House of Assembly of this province) of whom it may be truly said, that he was a kind husband, a tender parent, a sincere friend, and a *remarkable* lover of liberty, virtue, and his country. (Monday, December 31, 1750.)

On saturday morning died, much lamented, JOHN CHAMPNEYS, Esq; for some years Deputy-Secretary of this province. He was a man of a fair character, and consequently belov'd by all his acquaintance while here. (Ibid.)

On Thursday last died, much lamented, Mr. *Joseph Wragg*, son to the Hon. *Joseph Wragg*, Esq; (Monday, March 4, 1751.)

On Tuesday last, died, in the 81st Year of her Age, Mrs. *Elizabeth Smith*, who had lived upwards of *Seventy* Years in this Province, with an unblemished Reputation.—And some Months ago died also, in this Town, one Mrs. *Wilson*, said to be aged 109 Years:—Proofs that People may live to be as great Ages in

Carolina as in any Part of the World besides. (Monday, April 8, 1751.)

The same Night [Thursday] died, much lamented, the Honourable JOSEPH WRAGG, Esq; an eminent Merchant of this Town, who formerly dealt pretty largely in the Slave Trade, and had been many Years a Member of his Majesty's Council: His Character 'tis presumed is so well known, that we need say nothing of it here. (Monday, June 24, 1751.)

This Day died *Isaac Holmes*, Esq; lately appointed Member of his Majesty's Honourable Council. (Monday, November 25, 1751.)

Last Monday Night died, much lamented, after a lingering Indisposition, the Wife of *John Lloyd*, Esq; Commander of *Fort=Johnson*. (Monday, May 11, 1752.)

On Tuesday last died, in the 70th Year of his Age, *William Cattell*, Esq; one of the first Settlers and richest Men in this Province, who had lived retired some Years. (Monday, August 24, 1752.)

On Saturday Evening died, the Hon. JAMES GRÆME, Esq; who was Chief Justice of this Province, and Judge of the Court of Admiralty, and a Member of His Majesty's Council here. (Tuesday, September 1, 1752.)

From *Antigua*, we have had an Account of General MATTHEWS's Arrival; and of his Death in 3 Weeks thereafter, to the inexpressible Loss of the Island he came over to govern. (Tuesday, October 10, 1752.)

On the 31st past died, at *George-Town*, in the 19th Year of her Age, of a sore Throat, Mrs. *Sarah*, the Wife of Mr. *Joseph Brown* of that Place Merchant; and Daughter of *William Pinckney*, Esq; Deputy-Secretary: A young Lady of such valuable Accomplishments, that while her Neighbours and Acquaintance greatly lament their Loss, her Relations are almost inconsolable. (Monday, November 6, 1752.)

On Tuesday last died, after a lingering Indisposition, Mrs. *Mary Dart*, the Wife of *John Dart*, Esq; of this Town, Merchant: A Lady, that, for the many good Qualifications she possessed, was deservedly esteemed and is now universally lamented. (Monday, November 13, 1752.)

On Tuesday Morning the 21st Instant, died in the 78th Year of her Age, Mrs. *Isabella Wright*, Relict of the late Honourable *Robert Wright*, Esq; Chief Justice of this Province. (Monday, November 27, 1752.)

On Friday last died, Mrs. *Lois Matthewes*, in the 73d Year of her Age, 70 of which she has lived in this Province. (Monday, December 11, 1752.)

Yesterday died, universally lamented, Mrs. *Frances Elliott*, the Wife of *William Elliott*, Esq, A Lady that was possessed, to an eminent degree, of those valuable qualifications that rendered her justly and universally beloved, particularly by the *wise*, the *virtuous*, and the *indigent*. (Monday, December 18, 1752.)

On Friday Evening died Mrs. *Stone*, the Wife of Mr. *William Stone* Merchant, of this Town. (Monday, January 29, 1753.)

On Wednesday died Mr. *Edmond Larken*, Organist of *St. Philip's* Church in this Town. (Monday, February 5, 1753.)

On the 5th Instant died, universally lamented, the Rev. Mr. THOMAS MURRAY, Minister of the Gospel on *John's-Island*: As his ministerial Talents, chearful Conversation, steady Friendship, and unaffected Piety, commanded the Respect, and engaged the Affections, of all that knew him, his Death is not only a particular, but a public Loss. (Wednesday, August 15, 1753.)

From *Winyah*, we hear, that Mrs. *Smith*, the Wife of the Rev. Mr. *Michael Smith*, Rector of the Parish of *Prince Frederick*, died on the 16th ult. (Monday, August 27, 1753.)

Yesterday died. Sir *Alexander Nisbett*. (Monday, October 8, 1753.)

We hear from *Georgia*, that WILLIAM STEPHENS, Esq; lately died there, in the 83d Year of his Age (an Age to which few arrive in that Climate) who for many Years had made a considerable Figure in the polite World; had sat 26 Years in the British House of Commons, and, to his great Honor, in every Change, behaved with the greatest Steadiness and Truth to his Constituents. (Monday, October 22, 1753.)

On Thursday last died, at *Dorchester*, truly regretted by all that knew him, Doct. FREDERICK HOLZENDORF: a Man, whose Diligence and Care in his Vocation, as well as amiable Disposition, Behaviour and Character, had gain'd him the Esteem of every Individual: On Friday Evening he was decently interred, after the Manner of the *Free Masons*, many of whom attended the Funeral in Procession, during which Minute Guns were fired. He has left a disconsolate Widow, and a large Family of Children. (Tuesday, January 29, 1754.)

Last Wednesday Morning died, much lamented by all his Friends, Mr. *Henry Peronneau*, who after having acquired a very considerable Estate, retired from Business some Years since. (Tuesday, February 5, 1754.)

Last Sunday se'nnight died, aged 76 Years, Capt. *John Watson;* who had resided in this Province almost constantly from the *Third* Year of his Age, with an unblemished Character: But a few Days before his Death, as was his Custom every Morning, he walk'd from his House to Market, above half a Mile; and enjoyed all his Senses to a surprising Degree for a Man of his Age in *Carolina.* (Tuesday, March 5, 1754.)

Last Friday Evening died, universally lamented, Mrs. *Anne D'Harriette* (the Wife of Mr. *Benjamin D'Harriette*); who was a truly pious Christian, a most affectionate Wife, a tender Mother to the otherwise Motherless, a sincere Friend, and all that could render her respected. (Thursday, July 18, 1754.)

On Monday last died, of a Mortification, occasioned by the cutting of a Corn, the ingenious ALEXANDER GORDON, Esq; Clerk of His Majesty's Council in this Province[1]; which Office, we are informed, is now in the Hands of *William Simpson*, Esq. (Thursday, August 29, 1754.)

By Capt. *Lawrence* from *New-York*, we have an Account of the Death of *Robert Austin*, Esq; who went off for his Health, in the, *Shoreham* Man of War. By his Death, the Place of Controller of the Country Duties for this Port, is become vacant (Thursday, September 26, 1754.)

On the 11th Instant died, after a lingering Indisposition, Mr. *Benjamin Mathewes*, of this Town, Merchant,—who was, a most affectionate Husband, tender Parent, good Master, and sincere Friend. (Thursday, December 19, 1754.)

On Thursday last died, much lamented, Mr. ALEXANDER LIVIE, of this Town, Merchant. (Thursday, March 27, 1755.)

On Monday last died, Miss *Susannah Brewton*, a young Lady whose Death is truly lamented by all that knew her, as she was possessed of all those Qualifications that could render her respectable. (Thursday, September 11, 1755.)

Yesterday died, the Rev. Mr. *Henry Heywood*, a Baptist Preacher in this Town; who was esteemed one of the greatest Scholars in *America.* (Thursday, October 30, 1755.)

---

[1]This was the celebrated "Sandy" Gordon immortalized by Sir Walter Scott's "Jonathan Oldbuck" in "The Antiquary", but his taking off here in South Carolina was anything but romantic.

Yesterday died, the Honourable *Andrew Rutledge*, Esq; a Gentleman eminent for his Qualifications in the Practice of the Law, a benevolent and good Man, and who has several Times been chosen *Speaker* of the House of Assembly of this Province, where he always discharged his Trust with *Honour*: Hence, it cannot be doubted, that he was universally esteemed, and is universally lamented. (Thursday, November 20, 1755.)

On Tuesday died suddenly, Mr. *Benjamin d'Harriette*, formerly an eminent Merchant of this Town, but had retired from Business some Years—*knowing when he had enough*. We hear, he has bequeathed a considerable Legacy to the SOUTH CAROLINA SOCIETY. (Thursday, February 19, 1756.)

On Monday last died, of an apoplectic Fit, (as much regretted as he lived respected), *Anthony Matthewes*, Esq; a Native of this Province, aged 59 Years. (Thursday, August 26, 1756.)

On the 29th ult. died, Mrs. *Anne Dupont*, aged 81 Years, of which she had lived 68 in this Province, free from any Manner of Sickness (except what attends Child-bearing) 'till within 3 or 4 Years past; and walk'd about, and dined with the Family, the Day before she died. (Thursday, September 9, 1756—Supplement.)

Last Sunday Morning died, in the 71st Year of his Age, the Rev. Mr. *Alexander Garden*, formerly Rector of this Parish, and on Wednesday Morning he was privately interred agreeable to his own Request. (Saturday, October 2, 1756.)

On Tuesday died Capt. *William Thompson*, Master of the Snow *Elizabeth*, which lately put in here, and was bound for Jamaica from the Bay of Honduras. (Thursday, December 2, 1756.)

Last Sunday Night died, Mr. John Crockatt, formerly an eminent Merchant of this Town. (Friday, December 1, 1758.)

Tuesday Morning died, WALTER IZARD, Esq; who was possessed of one of the most considerable Fortunes in this Province, and a Representative in the present Assembly for the Parish of St. George, Dorchester. (Friday, January 19, 1759.)

And on Sunday last died Mr. *John Matthewes*. (Saturday, May 19, 1759.)

On Tuesday Night died suddenly, Mr. *Isaac Holmes* sen. (commonly called *Isaac Holmes* of *Church-Street*) remarkable for his uniform plainness and strict Honesty. (Saturday, August 11, 1759.)

Yesterday Morning died, in the 62d Year of his Age, *Robert Brewton*, Esq; Powder-Receiver of this Province; a Gentleman

who was deservedly esteemed and is sincerely regretted. **Mr.**
Jacob Motte, jun. is appointed to succeed him in his Office. (Saturday, August 18, 1759.)

On Tuesday last died, in the 47th Year of his Age, the Hon.
Peter Leigh, Esq; Chief-Justice of this Province, and Provincial Grand-Master of the Free and Accepted Masons. His public and private Character was such, that his Death is a sensible Loss to the Community, and to all who had any Connexion or Acquaintance with him, and will be long lamented. (Saturday, August 25, 1759.)

We hear from *Goose-Creek,* that last Sunday se'nnight died there, much lamented, Mrs. *Mary Taylor,* the Wife of *Peter Taylor,* Esq; a faithful and affectionate Consort, a sincere and valuable Friend and Neighbour, an agreeable Companion, a charitable and truly pious Christian; in few Words, a most excellent Woman. (Saturday, December 22, 1759.)

On Thursday last died here, in the 79th Year of his Age, Mr.
George Ducatt, who came into this Province a young Lad.
(Saturday, February 2, 1760.)

On the 8th Instant died, Mr. *Solomon Legaré,* sen. in the 87th Year of his Age, one of the oldest Settlers in this Province. He had been here 64 Years. And

On Tuesday last died at *Winyah,* the Hon. *John Cleland,* Esq; one of the Members of His Majesty's Hon. Council. (Saturday, May 24, 1760.)

On Tuesday last died, Daniel Crawford, Esq; one of the Five Representatives for this Town in the General Assembly. (Saturday, June 7, 1760.)

On sunday last died, very much lamented, *John Lining,* Esq; a gentleman eminent for his application and experience in discovering the causes, nature and cure of the disorders incident to this province, where he had practiced physic upwards of *twenty* years; and who possessed all the good qualifications that could render his loss great, as a physician, husband, father, master, friend, neighbour, companion, &c. (Saturday, September 27, 1760.)

On friday the 24th ult. died, in the 85th year of his age, doct.
Jacob Martin. (Saturday, November 1, 1760.)

The same day died, *Morton Brailsford,* Esq; controller of the country duties for the port of *Charles-Town;* to which office his honour the lieut. governor, the next day, appointed Mr. *Samuel Prioleau.* (Ibid.)

By Capt. *White*, from *London*, we have a confirmation of the death of the honourable *James Michie*, Esq; one of the members of his majesty's council for this province, chief justice, judge of his majesty's court of vice-admiralty, &c. &c. (Saturday, November 8, 1760.)

On tuesday died, the hon. *Thomas Drayton*, Esq; one of the members of his majesty's.council for this province; whose death, with the lieutenant-governor's preferment, the deaths of Mr. *Cleland* and Mr. *Michie*, and the resignation of Mr. *Saxby* and Mr. *Atkin*, makes six vacancies in the council. (Saturday, November 15, 1760.)

On saturday last died, ensign *Elrington*, of capt. *John Campbell's* company, in his majesty's XXIId regiment. (Saturday, February 14, 1761.)

Last saturday died, universally regretted by his congregation and all that knew him, the rev. Mr. WILLIAM HUTSON, pastor of the Independent Meeting in this town. (Saturday, April 18, 1761.)

And on Thursday died, Mr. *William Wilson*, Merchant, late a Co-partner of Mr. *Jennett*. (Saturday, May 9, 1761.)

Last night died *Childermas Croft*, Esq; many years clerk of the commons house of assembly of this province, for which place few were better qualified. 'Tis thought he will be succeeded by *Thomas Bromley*, Esq; who was lately appointed and sworn in clerk-assistant to that honourable house. (Saturday, May 16, 1761.)

On sunday last died, at *Savannah* in Georgia, lieut. *Lachlan Shaw*, of one of his majesty's independent companies in this province. He was esteemed a brave officer, and had particularly distinguished himself against the Rebels in the battle of *Culloden*. (Saturday, May 30, 1761.)

On Tuesday last died, Master Jordan Roche, only Son and Heir of Jordan Roche, Esq; deceased. (Saturday, August 8, 1761.)

On Wenesday the 30 ult. died here Mr. William Lloyd, merchant: And last Wednesday, Mr. Edward Newman, likewise of this town, merchant. (Saturday, October 10, 1761.)

On Thursday the 8th instant died, at Mars Bluff in Craven county, the Hon. Edmond Atkin, Esq; his Majesty's superintendant of Indian affairs in the southern department of North-America. (Saturday, October 17, 1761.)

On the 27th ult. died, at Savannah in Georgia, universally regretted, Mrs. Robinson, the wife of the hon. Pickering Robinson, Esq; (Saturday, November 14, 1761.)

On Friday the 27th ult. died, Mrs. Mary Brewton, widow of the late Robert Brewton, Esq; (Saturday, December 5, 1761.)

On the 18th instant died, at Sophia-Hall, Mr. Andrew Fesch, merchant. (Saturday, January 9, 1762.)

On Monday last departed this life, the rev. Mr. Jonathan Copp, rector of St. John's parish in Colleton county, much regretted. (Saturday, January 9, 1762.)

In the Paragraph in our last which mentions Mr. Fesch's death, for instant, *read* ultimo. (Saturday, January 9, 1762.)

On Thursday night died, Mr. John Gordon, tavern-keeper; remarkable for his honesty and good-nature, and keeping the best house of publick entertainment in America. (Saturday, January 16, 1762.)

On Sunday last died, Capt. James Rodger, upwards of 20 years a commander in this trade, wherein he acquired a handsome fortune with a fair character. (Saturday, January 23, 1762.)

On Sunday last died, in the 67th year of age, Mr. Henry Bedon, a native of this province, and a hearty man till a little time before his death: A brother of this gentleman, aged 74 years, likewise a native of this province, died here about four years ago. These are proofs of the sanity of this country, and that people can live to a good old age as well as any where else. (Saturday, March 6, 1762.)

On Wednesday last died Mrs. Elizabeth Wooddrop, the wife of Mr. William Wooddrop. And,

On Friday, Mr. Thomas White, of Monck's Corner, merchant. (Monday, August 23, 1762—postscript to Saturday, August 21, 1762.)

On Wednesday last died capt. William Benson, commander of the Marlborough, of Liverpoole, lately arrived here from Africa. (Saturday, September 25, 1762.)

On Tuesday morning died, as much lamented at his death as respected while living, John McQueen, Esq; a very eminent merchant here. (Saturday, November 13, 1762.)

Last Friday died, most justly lamented, Mr. Job Milner, merchant, remarkable for his benevolence and strict adherence to the social duties. (Saturday, January 15, 1763.)

Yesterday died Capt. Samuel Liddal, master and owner of the

ship Peggy of Skields, which arrived here the day before from Lisbon. (Saturday, April 23, 1763.)

The same day [the Sunday before] died, Miss Judith Fraser, sister to Alexander Fraser, Esq; (Saturday, May 7, 1763.)

On saturday last died, in the seventy-first year of her age, Mrs. Mary Blamyer, a native of this province. And,

On wednesday died, aged 72 (some say nearer 80) years, Alexander Stewart, Esq; who came over here in or about the year 1715, and has acted many years as a magistrate and register of his majesty's court of chancery. (Saturday, May 21, 1763.)

There is advice, from London, of the death of the following persons, viz.

Mrs. Abigail Watsone, the wife of Mr. John Watsone, formerly of this province, but now of London, merchant.

Mrs. Anne Gibbes, the wife of Mr. Robert Gibbes of John's Island, who went to England last year for her health.

Mrs. Balgay, sister to Thomas Wright, Esq; And,

Mrs. Mary Taylor (the wife of Mr. John Taylor) who kept the Pennsylvania, Carolina, and Georgia coffee-house in Birchin-Lane, London. (Ibid.)

On Tuesday night died, of the Small-pox, Miss Anne Matthewes, only daughter of the late Benj Matthewes, Esq. (Saturday, June 25, 1763.)

"Last Sunday died, much lamented by his Congregation and all that knew him, and in the 64th Year of his Age, the Rev. Mr. John-James Tissot, near 34 Years Pastor of the French Church in the Parish of St. Thomas & St. Dennis." (Saturday, July 9, 1763.)

Last thursday morning died, Mr. Thomas Batty, of this town, merchant, and only son of Mr. Batty at Leeds in Yorkshire. (Saturday, August 6, 1763.)

On sunday last died, at Winyah, Col. Daniel Horry. (Saturday, September 17, 1763.)

On the 17th ult. died in this town, Mr. Thomas Lining, cabinet-maker; on the 21st, Mr. John Thomson, merchant, copartner with Mr. James Hunter; and on the 24th, Mrs. Rebecca Guthrie. (Saturday, October 1, 1763.)

On the 6th instant, died at sea, in the 63d year of his age (on his return from Rhode-Island, whither he lately went for the recovery of his health) Ebenezer Simmons, sen. Esq. And

On the 11th died, Mrs. Anne Roche, the wife of Mr. Francis

Roche, and daughter of the said Mr. Simmons. (Saturday, October 15, 1763.)

On the 13th also died, Mr. John Afline, of this town, merchant. (Ibid.)

The same evening [the Sunday before] died, in the 73d year of his age, Mr. *Thomas Bolton*, who came to this province with governor *Nicholson* in 1721. (Saturday, November 26, 1763.)

Last tuesday died, Mr. Archibald Johnston, one of the first, best, and most considerable Indico-makers, in this province. (Saturday, December 17, 1763.)

This morning also died, Mr. Isaac Holmes, of this town, merchant, lately returned from England. (Ibid.)

Yesterday morning died, suddenly, at George-Town, Winyah, Mr. Andrew Johnston; brother to Archibald Johnston, Esq; who also died suddenly here the 13th ult. (Saturday, January 7, 1764.)

[June] 16th, Died, Mrs. Mary Mazyck, the wife of Isaac Mazyck, Esq; (Monday, October 8, 1764.)

[September] 6th, Died in *St. John's* parish, *Berkley* county, Major *René Ravenell*, aged 72 years; and about the same time, Mrs. *Catharine Cordes*, relict of the late Col. *Thomas Cordes*, aged 64; (Ibid.)

[September] 22d. Died Mrs. *Martha Grimke*, wife of *Frederick Grimke*, Esq; (Ibid.)

On Sunday last died, Alexander Broughton, Esq; (Monday, October 8, 1764.)

On Saturday night last died, Mr. JOHN BALL, an eminent planter, in St. John's Parish. (Monday, October 22, 1764.)

On the 23d ult. died at Stono, aged 77 years, Mrs. *Mary Miles*, born in America, and who had lives 57 years in this province. Her husband, Mr. *Thomas Miles*, a native of this province, died 5 years ago, in the 71st year of his age. The generation of this pair, was 9 children, 57 grand children, and 12 great-grand-children, in all 79; of which there now remain alive, 3 children, 23 grand-children, and 7 great-grand-children. (Monday, November 5, 1764.)

This morning died, *John Raven*, Esq; formerly a member of the commons house of assembly of this province. (Monday, December 3, 1764.)

On monday last died, Mr. Robert Mackewn, jun. And

On tuesday, at his plantation on John's-Island, Col. John
Gibbes, a native of this province, aged 59 years. (Monday, December 24, 1764.)

Last Thursday night died, aged 87 years, Mr. GEORGE DAN-
DRIDGE, who had lived near fifty years in this province.

And, "early on Friday morning also died, Mrs. MARY SMYTH.
the wife of Mr. ROBERT SMYTH, merchant, a most amiable
woman, in whom were conspicuous the ditiful and affectionate
wife, the tender and indulgent mother, the kind mistress, the
sincere and valuable friend, and the pious Christian. As her
life was always calm and easy, and her disposition chearful, so
she departed this life with the fortitude becoming a good
Christian." (Saturday, January 26, 1765.)

On Tuesday last died, Mr. Thomas Lamboll, only son of
Thomas Lamboll, Esq. (Saturday, February 9, 1765.)

On Wednesday last died Mr. John Simmons, eldest son of the
late Ebenezer Simmons, Esq.

The same died Mrs. Ruth Bedon, relict of the late Mr. Stephen
Bedon, junior. (Saturday, March 9, 1765.)

The 27th ult. died of an apoplectick fit, at Augusta in Georgia,
Mr. Nicholas Cashel, than whom perhaps few *there* ever were
more regretted; for, though he was not without a fault, yet was
he possessed of many virtues, such as, honour and honesty, a
forgiving temper, and a heart full of tenderness to the distressed, whom he always liberally relieved and assisted; he was
also an affectionate husband, tender parent, and kind master.
His remains were interred the 28th, with all the honours the
place would admit. From the time of his decease to the interment of his corpse, the flag at Mr. Macartan's fort was hoisted
half staff, and minute guns were fired there, for an hour and a
half, during the funeral procession. The pallbearers, &c. wore
linnen scarfs and cambrick hatbands, agreeable to the laudable
custom in Ireland on such occasions. (Supplement to Saturday,
March 9, 1765.)

Yesterday died in the 65th year of her age, Mrs. Anne Austin,
the wife of George Austin, Esq; at present in England.

And last night also died, James Grindlay, Esq; attorney at
law. (Saturday, June 8, 1765.)

Tuesday last died at St. Augustine, the Honourable James
Moultrie, Esq; Chief-Justice of East-Florida, and son to John
Moultrie, sen, Esq; of this town.

Last night died, Mrs. Martha Chalmers, the wife of Doctor Lionel Chalmers. (Saturday, August 10, 1765.)

Last Thursday morning died, after a short illness, much regretted by his acquaintance, THOMAS BROMLEY, Esq; clerk assistant to the hon. commons house of assembly of this province; and the next day his remains were interred, without any funeral pomp, agreeable to his own request; on the plantation of Peter Manigault, Esq; at Goose-Creek, attended by a number of his particular friends. (Monday, August 26, 1765.)

Tuesday last died, at Goose-Creek, in the 65th year of his age, the last 40 of which he lived in this colony, Peter Taylor, Esq; a native of Ireland, formerly commissary-general, and a gentleman universally beloved.

Wednesday died in the 85th year of her age, the last 50 of which she lived in this town, Mrs. Anne Milner, a native of Bermuda—one who, while she was able, delighted in doing good to the poor. (Saturday, October 5, 1765.)

Friday morning died, William Raven, Esq. (Saturday, October 19, 1765.)

From East-Florida, we have an account of the deaths of Dennis Rolle, Esq; member of parliament for Barnstaple, and Harry Lloyd, Esq. (Thursday, October 31, 1765.)

Yesterday died, much regretted, Miss *Elizabeth Banbury.* (Monday, July 14, 1766.)

Tuesday last died much regretted, the facetious Capt. ROBERT BOYD, aged 44 years: He was second Captain of the Artillery Company, and buried with military honours. (Monday, July 21, 1766.)

The 20th past died suddenly, near *Augusta,* Lieut. *Theodore Frederic Winter,* of the Royal American regiment, who commanded there 'till Mr. *Keough* was ordered thither.

About the same time died, at *Strawberry, Shepard Eustace,* master of the Brigt. *Philadelphia-Packet,* of *Bristol.*

Last Tuesday died here, after a very short illness, *Richard Black,* Esq; Collector of His Majesty's Customs at *Beaufort* in this province,—a gentleman who was deservedly much esteemed, and is now much regretted. (Monday, August 11, 1766.)

Wednesday last died, Col. William Walter. (Monday, August 18, 1766.)

On Tuesday died, Mr. Christopher Gadsden, jun. a very promising youth, oldest son to Christopher Gadsden, Esq. (Monday, August 25, 1766.)

Tuesday last died suddenly, Mr. Thomas Lloyd (of Georgia), merchant. (Monday, September 8, 1766.)

Yesterday morning died after a lingering indisposition, John Denton, Esq; one of the searchers of his Majesty's customs of this port. (Monday, September 15, 1766.)

Yesterday died, much regretted by every one who knew him, Mr. George Blaikie, Cooper, lately returned from Britain, whither he went for the Recovery of his Health. (Monday, January 2, 1775.)

Last Monday died, in Childbed, Mrs. Elizabeth Shepheard, the Wife of Mr. Charles Shepheard, Merchant, and only Daughter of Mr. Thomas Ratcliffe. (Monday, February 13, 1775.)

On Wednesday last died Mrs. Penelope Brown, Sister to the Hon. Rawlins Lowndes, Speaker of the present Hon. Commons House of Assembly of this Province, who lately arrived here on a Visit to her Brother.

The same Day died, Miss Sally Burrows, youngest Daughter of William Burrows, Esq; Master in Chancery; and this Morning, Mrs. Mary Burrows, the Wife of the said Mr. Burrows. (Monday, February 13, 1775.)

Last Thursday died, supposed to be upwards of 80 Years of Age, Mr. James McAlpine, formerly esteemed an eminent Teacher of Music here. It is said he arrived in this Colony at the age of 19 Years. (Monday, February 20, 1775.)

On Saturday Evening died, much lamented by all that were acquainted with her, Mrs. Providence Prioleau, the Wife of Samuel Prioleau, Esq; a great Part of whose Life was spent in Acts of Beneficence to the Poor, and in affording Assistance and Relief to the Sick of all Sorts. (Monday, February 20, 1775.)

"On Wednesday died, in the 31st Year of her Age, Mrs. Elizabeth Macpherson, the amiable Consort of Isaac Macpherson, Esq.—justly lamented by all who had the Pleasure of her Acquaintance—as she was, a devout Christian, an affectionate Wife, a tender Parent, a sincere Friend, and always ready to relieve the Wretched and Indigent." (Monday, March 27, 1775.)

On Sunday last, as Charles Beck, a Servant to Mr. Kalteisen, of this Town, was attempting to ride thro' Ashley-River, at the Ferry, he was unfortunately drown'd; the Horse gained the opposite Shore. (Tuesday, September 26, 1775.)

INDEX.

Death Notices
In The South Carolina Gazette, 1766-1774

CONTRIBUTED TO
The South Carolina Historical and Genealogical Magazine
BY MABEL L. WEBBER

DEATH NOTICES FROM THE SOUTH CAROLINA GAZETTE FROM SEPTEMBER 29, 1766 TO DECEMBER 19, 1774

Contributed by MABEL L. WEBBER

These death notices fill in the gap in the *Death Notices in the South Carolina Gazette 1732–1775*, compiled and edited by A. S. Salley Jr., and published by the Historical Commission of South Carolina in 1917. The omission occurs between September 15, 1766, and January 2, 1775, and was due to the carelessness of the printer in losing the copy of the notices taken from the intervening issues of the *Gazette*.

Last Monday died at Beaufort, much lamented, Mr. Francis Smart, merchant there, and brother to the Superintendent of Indian affairs for the Southern department of America. (Monday, September 29, 1766.)

Monday last died, Capt. John M'Cleish, Master of the Sloop Fanny. —and, on Tuesday, at Stono, aged 67, Mr. Robert Mackewn, a Native of this Province. (Monday Oct. 6, 1766.)

Saturday the 4th Instant died at Stono, greatly lamented by all who had the pleasure of her acquaintance Mrs. Anne Tonge, the Wife of the Reverend Mr. John Tonge, Rector of St. Pauls Parish.

Wednesday last died, aged 77 Years, Mrs. Mary Heskett, Widow, who had lived in this Town about 55 Years.

Yesterday died Mrs. Mary Frost, aged 79 Years, who came to this Province from New England in the Year 1714.

This morning died said to be 67 Years, the Honourable Hector Bellinger [(*sic*) Beranger is the name] De Beaufain, Esq; Fellow of the Royal Society, formerly a Member of His Majesty's Council, and 24 Years Collector of His Majesty's Customs in this Province—The least we can say of him is, that he has not left a Superior Character in the Universe, nor many equal. [Account of his funeral in the next issue.] Long-Canes, Sept. 24, 1766

Of a Miscarriage of Twins, on the 10th Instant, died here in the 24th Year of her àge, one of the most pious and accomplished young Women of these parts, in the person of Mrs. Calhoun, the Wife of Patrick Calhoun Esq; and Daughter of the Rev. Mr. Alexander Craighead. (Monday, Oct. 13, 1766.)

1

From (Port Royal) We hear that about a fortnight since died, at the advanced age of 87, Years, Mrs. Reynolds, a native of this Province.

Last night died, Mrs. Agnes Lind, Milliner, a very industrious good woman, the Wife of Mr. Thomas Lind.

Wednesday last died, much lamented by all that had an acquaintance with him, but more particularly by the Parish of St. James Goose Creek, which he had represented in the Assembly of this Province, and to which (as he resided there) he was very useful and a great benefactor, Robert Hume Esq; aged 37. Men of his character and disposition when they die, are always a public loss. (Monday Oct. 27, 1766.)

Saturday the 1st Instant died at Beaufort, Port-Royal, Capt. George Perkins, master of the ship St. Helena, lately launched there. (Monday, Nov. 10, 1766.)

Last Tuesday night died, Mr. William Watson, lately arrived here from England, and son of the late Mr. John Watson, of London, formerly of this place, merchant. (Monday, Nov. 17, 1766.)

Friday night died, aged 70 years, William Elliott, Esq; as hearty a man as most of 40 years of age, and a native of this province.

This morning died, Capt Silas Miles, of St. Paul's parish. (Monday, Dec. 1, 1766.)

Tuesday last died aged 63 years, after a very tedious indisposition, William Pinckney, Esq; Commissary-general, (and a native) of this province. 'Tis said, Benjamin Simons Esq; will be appointed to succeed MR. Pinckney as commissary-general. (Monday, Dec. 8, 1766.)

Tuesday last died, greatly lamented, aged 73 years, Mrs. Elizabeth Hunt, a native of this province, and practising mid-wife.—It is said to appear from an account regularly kept by her, that she had been present at the birth of near 4000 children. She was remarkably strong and healthy, till within a few months before her death, and, had she taken common care of her constitution, promised very fair to have lived beyond the century. (Monday, Dec., 22, 1766)

Yesterday died suddenly, at his plantation near Dorchester, Adam Daniel, Esq., and

Last night, near 70 years of age, Mr. Edward Bullard, of this town, always remarkably strong, hearty and chearful, till within a fortnight of his decease. (Monday, Jan. 19, 1767)

Tuesday, the 20th inst. died in St. Thomas' Parish, at the advanced age of 77 years, Mrs. Mary-Ann Bourdeaux, a native of this Province. (Monday, Jan. 26, 1767.)

Last Monday night died, Mr. Caleb Lloyd, Merchant, and co-partner with Mr. John Neyle. This gentleman's character and disposition were so amiable, that his friends sustain a particular loss in his death, which would have been generally lamented, but for the prejudices that were conceived against him, upon his being unhappily appointed Distributor of Stamps in this Province, under the late Act of the British Parliament that proved so universally odious and detestable to all America, even where a suspension of its operation could not be procured. (Monday, Feb. 16, 1767)

On the 1st instant died, at her plantation near Ashley-Ferry, upwards of 80 years of age, Mrs. Margaret Ladson, a native of this province, and a daughter of Mr. Daniel Donovan, who was one of the first settlers, and remarkably distinguished himself by the gallant defence he made against the Indians, during the war with those people, which begun in the year 1715, and the use he made on that occasion of some dogs which he brought with him from Ireland. (Monday, March 16, 1767)

At a Court of General Sessions of the Peace-Oyer and Terminer, Assize and General Goal Delivery, which was opened on the 18th past, and ended the 25th, the following persons were capitally convicted, viz:

Antonio Christian: of Murder.

. . . .

Christian was hanged the 31st instant. The others were pardoned by His Majesty. (Monday, April 13, 1767)

The 30th past died, in this town, William Branford, Esq. reckoned one of the best planters in this province. (Monday, May 11, 1767)

Wednesday last died, Mr. William Kelly, one of the Branch Pilots for the Bar and Harbour of Charles Town.

The same day the Body of James Riggs, an Apprentice Lad to Captain Peter Mallet, who had been missing two Days, floated up into Col. Beale's Dock, being cut under his Chin from Ear to Ear: A jury of Inquest sat on the Body, and next day brought in their Verdict of Wilful Murder by Persons unknown; since which, two

Apprentice Lads have been committed to Jail on Suspicion of being the Perpetrators. (Monday, June 29, 1767)

Last Monday, died suddenly, Capt. George Spender, late master of the ship Katharine, of London. (Monday, July 6, 1767)

. . . . Last Thursday died Mr. George Marshall, having survived his wife only a few weeks. As a very honest man, which was his character, his death is much regretted by all who knew him. (Monday, July 20, 1767)

Last Tuesday evening, one Sullivan, a Ship Carpenter, was shot through the body and killed on the spot, on the high road, about half a mile without the town, by one Floyd, a Clock-Maker. The Jury of inquest brought in their verdict of Wilful murder, and Floyd is committed to jail, to be tried at next October sessions. (Monday, Aug. 3, 1767)

Saturday sennight died, at his plantation in Prince William's Parish, aged 72 years, capt. John Bull, brother to the late, and uncle to the present Lieutenant governor of this province.

Yesterday died Mrs. Anne Matthewes, wife of Mr. John Matthewes (son of James). (Monday, August 24, 1767)

On Friday night died, aged 79 years, Mr. Adam Stewart, who had resided near sixty years in this province, and was in the vessel that took Major Stede Bonnet, the pirate, who with his crew were executed here about fifty years ago. (Monday, Aug. 31, 1767)

Sunday the 30th past, died, Mrs. Peronneau, relict of the late Henry Peronneau, Esq. (Monday, Sept. 7, 1767)

Saturday last died, Mr. Balguy Littlewood, merchant. (Monday, Sept. 14, 1767)

The 9th instant died here, lieut. George Towers; and on the 14th Mr. William Grant, pursar, both of his Majesty's ship, Sardoine, commanded by Capt. James Hawker. (Monday, Sept. 21, 1767)

Last Tuesday died, just seven weeks after his marriage to Miss Angelica Le Tour, Mr. Francis Virambaut, aged 68 years.

On Friday night died, Mr. John Neyle, merchant. (Monday, Sept. 28, 1767)

The 21st past, died at Savannah, in Georgia, Thomas Vincent, Esq. one of the Representatives for that town, in the assembly of that province. (Monday, Oct. 5, 1767)

Last Tuesday died, universally regretted, that truly pious and good man, the Rev. Mr. Joseph Dacre Appleby Wilton, assistant lecturer to the rector of the parish of St. Philip; by whose death, the united voice of all ranks of people in this town, and of every one who had any connexion or acquaintance with him justify us in saying, the public has sustained an irreparable loss. (Monday, Oct. 12, 1767)

Monday last, died, after a short illness, the humane, social and friendly Doctor William Pillans, who was very useful in his profession, and had he lived, would have become eminent in it.

On Saturday, the 26th past, died at Beaufort, Port Royal, Mrs. Eleanor Proctor; a lady universally regretted by all who had the pleasure of her acquaintance, and particularly lamented by her intimates. (Monday, Oct. 19, 1767)

Wednesday last died that truly pious and good man, the Rev. Mr. Daniel Wheeler, minister of the society or congregation distinguished by the name of general Baptists.

Last Monday morning died, Mrs. Susannah Scott, aged 75 years. She was brought to this Province from New England, at about 5 years of age. (Monday, Nov. 16, 1767)

Saturday night died, Mrs. Anne Outerbridge, the wife of Capt. White Outerbridge. (Monday, Nov. 23, 1767)

Last night died Mr. Francis Lee, of Georgia. (Monday, Nov. 30, 1767)

On Friday last, died Mr. William Townsend, of John's Island. (Monday, Dec. 7, 1767)

On Wednesday died Mrs. Elizabeth Lord, the wife of Mr. Andrew Lord, and sister to Mr. Greenwood, merchant in London. (Monday Dec. 14, 1767)

Last Monday night died, much lamented, Mrs. Mary Wragg, the wife of William Wragg, esq., and was, agreeable to her own request, interred without any funeral pomp, on Thursday following. (Monday, Jan. 4, 1768)

This morning died, the right honourable Lady Anne, one of the daughters of the Earl of Cromartie, formerly married to the honourable Edward Atkin, Esq. Superintendent of Indian Affairs for the Southern Department of North America, and since his decease to John Murray, Esq. M.D. (Monday, Jan. 18, 1768)

Last Friday died, after a long and severe indisposition, and universally regretted, Mrs. Mary Gadsden, the wife of Christopher Gadsden, Esq.

Tuesday last died, aged 64 years, George Seaman, Esq.; who formerly was an eminent merchant here, but had retired from business. (Monday, Feb. 2, 1768)

Yesterday died, Mr. Richard Downes, jun. Merchant, of Dorchester. (Monday, Feb. 16, 1768)

Last friday night died, the hon. Charles Shinner Esq. a.member of His Majesty's Council, and late chief justice of this province. His lady, and both his children, died some time before him. (Monday, Feb. 29, 1768)

The 13th past died, at Pine-Tree Hill, Samuel Wyly, Esq.

On Saturday died, Mr. Alexander Petrie. (Monday, March 7, 1768)

Last Tuesday night, as Capt. Richard Davis, of the Ship Hope, was going on board, he fell off the stage and was drowned. (Monday, March 21, 1768)

On Wednesday last died, William Middleton, Esq. eldest son of Colonel Thomas Middleton, deceased, and a representative in the present assembly for the parish of St. Helena. (Monday, Apl. 11, 1768)

On Tuesday last, died, in the 69th year of her age, Mrs. Sarah Stoutenburgh, a native of this province, and relict of the late Mr. Luke Stoutenburgh. (Monday, Apl. 18, 1768)

Last Saturday died, Mr. James Streater, aged 76 years.

Also Mr. William Dandridge, aged 47. (Monday, May 2, 1768) Thursday last died, Mrs. Sarah Skirving, the wife of James Skirving, Esq.; (formerly Mrs. Champneys)

Yesterday morning died, after a tedious and lingering illness, Mrs. Elizabeth Pinckney, the wife of Roger Pinckney, Esq. Provost Marshal of this Province. (Monday, Aug. 15, 1768)

The Rev. Mr. James Crallan, late Master of the Free School here, and Assistant-Lecturer for St. Philip's Parish, died the twelfth day after he went to Sea on his passage for England. (Monday, Aug. 29, 1768)

On Thursday died, Mrs. Elizabeth Mullins, the wife of Mr. George Mullins of St. Paul's Parish. (Monday, Sept. 19, 1768)

Last friday night died, Capt. Henry Richardson, of this town, and

last night died, Mrs. Anne Howarth, the wife of Colonel Probart Howarth, commander of Fort Johnson—as universally regretted

---

dead as esteemed *living*, by all her friends and acquaintances. (Monday, Sept. 26, 1768)

Last Monday at 8 o'clock in the evening died, (greatly lamented by all who knew her) after a lingering illness, which she bore with, great resignation, Mrs. Elizabeth Elliott, (relict of the late Barnard Elliott, Esq.) aged 51 years and 7 months. (Monday, Oct. 3, 1768)

This day died, Mr. Samuel Peronneau, Merchant. (Monday, Oct. 17, 1768)

Tuesday last died, Mr. James O'Brian, attorney at law.

A few days before, died Mr. Bennett Oldham, of the same profession.

Last Wednesday died, after a lingering indisposition, Mr. George Bedon, merchant, son of Henry.

And on Saturday night died suddenly, Mrs. Anne Child, relict, of the late Mr. Joseph Child, of Ashley-River.

On Tuesday, the 18th instant, died at St. Augustine, much lamented, William Greening, Esq. naval officer, and register of grants in East-Florida, and formerly post-master there—a gentleman of most amiable character.

The honourable William Simpson, Esq. Chief Justice of Georgia, died there last week. (Monday, Oct. 24, 1768)

Thursday last died, Mr. Ezekiel David, Merchant. (Monday Oct. 31, 1768)

Last Saturday night died, Captain William Kenny, of the Ship Amity's Advice, which put in here the 18th past in distress, from Jamaica, bound for London. (Monday, Nov. 7, 1768)

Thursday last departed this life, in the 42nd year of his age, much lamented, the ingenious Mr. William Johnson (well known in America by his Lectures and Experiments in Electricity, and here, by the excellent plan he had formed for an English School) whose death may be justly reckoned a loss to the public, and is an irreparable one to his family.

The 26th past died, Mr. George Livingston, an eminent Factor in his town.

On Monday night died here, Mr. Robert Davies, in the 108th year of his age. (Thursday, Jan. 5, 1769)

(To be continued)

DEATH NOTICES FROM THE SOUTH CAROLINA GAZETTE FROM SEPTEMBER 29, 1766 TO DECEMBER 19, 1774

Contributed by MABEL L. WEBBER

(Continued from January)

Last Monday died, Mr. George Gordon, of Jamaica, who lately came here for the recovery of his health. (Thursday, Jan. 5, 1769.)

On Sunday last died, in the 90th year of her age, having lived upwards of 50 years in this province, Mrs. Ann Peacock, relict of Mr. Peacock, who died about 30 years ago. (Thursday, Jan. 12, 1769.)

Yesterday morning died at Dorchester, Mrs. Mary McNeill, the amiable consort of Doct. Archibald McNeill. (Thursday, Jan. 19, 1769.)

Last Friday died Mrs. Frances Prue, the Wife of Mr. John Prue, whose Funeral was conducted in the same Manner as the late Mrs. Gadsden's. (Monday, Feb. 16, 1769.)

Last Saturday evening, between 7 and 8 o'clock a most melancholy accident happened here, viz: A sailing boat returning from Hobcaw, in which were Capt. George Higgins of the Snow Portland, Mr. Thomas Coleman, upholsterer, Mr. John Hill, (who lived at Mr. Paul Townsend's) Mr. Thomas Gunter, an apprentice to Capt. Higgins, two negro men, and a negro boy, by some mismanagement in a sudden squall of wind, filled, and sunk, off Capt. Gadsden's Wharf, whereby Capt. Higgins, Mr. Coleman, Mr. Hill, and one of the negro men lost their lives. The rest were with some difficulty saved, as they drove by some vessels in the stream before the town. Neither the boat, nor any of the drowned have yet been found. The unfortunate Capt. Higgins, who had been married only three weeks before this catastrophe, is particularly regretted.

Last Monday morning died, John Cattell, Esq. of Wampee-Savannah, captain of the St. George's troop of horse. (Thursday, March 9, 1769.)

8

On the 5th instant died, in Prince William's Parish, of which he was an inhabitant, truly and greatly regretted. Mr. Robert McLeod, merchant; who, by his upright and friendly behavior, was much esteemed by the many that had the pleasure of his acquaintance. (Thursday, March 16, 1769.)

Last Friday night died, Capt. James Rodgers, formerly a Branch-Pilot for this Port and Harbour, afterwards, in the last war, commander of a privateer fitted out here, and since master of different vessels in the merchant service. He was remarkable for his bravery, and not less so for strict honour in all his dealing; but he was left an almost helpless family.

The same day the body of Mr. Thomas Coleman, one of the unfortunate persons drowned on the 4th instant, was found near Capt. Lempriere's point, and on Saturday brought to town, where, after a jury had made the necessary inquisition, it was decently interred, the Fellowship and Recess Societies attending the funeral. Last Monday the body of Mr. John Hill was likewise found, near the same place, brought to town, and buried as the former. The body of Captain George Higgins has not yet been found, nor is the boat wherein the three were drowned. (Thursday, March 23, 1769.)

Friday last, the body of the unfortunate Captain Higgins, was taken up, in the river, and the next day decently interred; most of the respectable inhabitants of the town attending the funeral, as a mark of the particular respect they bore to that worthy man when living. (Thursday, March 30, 1769.)

Last Tuesday Morning, died, Mrs. Martha Bremar, Widow of the late Mr. Francis Bremar.

The same day died, Peter Broughton, Esq. of St. John's Parish. (Thursday, May 11, 1769.)

Last Saturday died the eldest daughter of His Excellency the Right Honourable Lord Charles-Greville Montagu, Governor in Chief, etc. of this Province. And the next day His Excellency returned from his Journey to the Western Frontiers.

On Wednesday the 17th inst. died Capt. James Caird, Master of the Brigantine Ashton, of Liverpoole.

Last Friday died here, Mrs. Jane Douxsaint, a Native of this Province, aged 73 years. (Thursday, May 25, 1769.)

On Sunday last died, aged 53 years, Mrs. Susannah Bee, Relict of the late Colonel John Bee; a Lady of so amiable and exemplary a disposition, as renders her Death a Loss to Society. (Thursday, June 15, 1769.)

Sunday last died, much regretted by those who knew him, Mr. Christopher Simpson, merchant.

Last Monday died, Mr. John St. Leger, Attorney at Law. (Thursday, June 29, 1769.)

Last Sunday morning died, a Batchelor, aged 51 Years, Mr. George Matthewes, who had many good Qualities, and has left a considerable Fortune—No Scarves were given at his funeral, nor, (as we hear) was any New Mourning bought, tho' the Train of Relations that attended his Funeral was very considerable. (Thursday, July 13, 1769.)

Last Saturday died, Mrs. Catharine Waring, wife of Mr. Waring. (Thursday, July 27, 1769.)

Last Night died Mr. James Sands, merchant. (Monday, Aug. 3, 1769.)

Last Monday died, Mr. Thomas Lee, Carpenter, aged fifty-nine years, thirty-five of which he has lived in this Town. (Thursday, Aug. 10, 1769.)

Yesterday se'nnight died, upwards of 75 years of Age, and a Native of this Province, Mrs. Rachel Howard, the Widow of Mr. Experience Howard, who died many years ago. (Thursday, Aug. 17, 1769.)

The same Day died, Mrs. Elizabeth Clitherall, the Wife of Dr. James Clitherall. (Thursday, Aug. 31, 1769.)

Last Friday died Thomas Smith, sen. Esq. aged 74 years, most of which he had lived in this Province.

Last Monday died the amiable consort of Mr. Thomas Walter, Merchant.

The same died, the Rev. Mr. Farmer, Rector of St. John's Parish, Berkley County, universally regretted by his parishoners, and all that had the Pleasure of an Acquaintance with him. (Thursday, Sept. 14, 1769.)

On Thursday last died, Mrs. Ann Ward, the Wife of Mr. John Ward, Taylor. (Thursday, Sept. 21, 1769.)

Last Saturday Evening died, Mr. Joseph Ball, sen. of this Town, aged 66 years. (Thursday, Sept. 28, 1769.)

Last Sunday died, Mrs. Isabella Wish, the wife of Mr. John Wish. (Thursday, Oct. 5, 1769.)

On Friday last died, much regretted, Mr. James Reid, of Pon Pon, who was one of the representatives of the Parish of St. Bartholomew, in the present General Assembly.

The same Day also died suddenly, aged 67 years, Captain Edward Lightwood, many Years Gunner of Charles Town. (Thursday, Oct. 18, 1769.)

On Thursday last died, Mrs. Marion Charlotte Porcher, the last of six children left by Mr. Philip Gendron, one of the first French Protestants that arrived and settled at Santee, in this Province, about the year 1685, and who died about the year 1725. The following is an account of their Births, Deaths and Ages:

	Born	Died	Age
John Gendron	Oct. 12, 1690	1754	64
Magdalen Prioleau	Oct. 13, 1691	1765	74
Elizabeth Huger	Oct. 14, 1692	1740	48
Marian Charlotte Porcher	Feb. 21, 1694–5	1769	74
Jane Douxsaint	May 19, 1696	1769	63
Catharine-Henrietta Cordes	Apl. 12, 1696	1764	68
	(sic)		

(Thursday, Oct. 26, 1769.)

Last Tuesday, died, universally regretted, on his Plantation at Combahee, of a nervous Fever, and after a short illness, William Ward Crosthwate, Esq. formerly of the Army, aged only Twenty-six years. (Thursday, Nov. 2, 1769.)

Last Saturday morning died, much regretted by the Gentlemen of the Turf, and all his Acquaintance, Mr. Thomas Nightingale, who has for several years past kept the House and Course called New-Market.

On Sunday Night died, Mr. David Stoddard, Merchant.

Last Tuesday died Mrs. Elizabeth Williams, Wife of Robert Williams, jun, esq.

The humorous Mr. John Snelling, and Mr. James Duthie.

Died, Nov. 9th, Mrs. Patience Catharine Stevens, Wife of Mr. Daniel Stevens, after a long and lingering illness, which she bore with steady patience, and Christian Resignation. (Thursday, Nov. 9, 1769.)

On Tuesday last died, Mrs. Elizabeth Fuller, wife of Thomas Fuller, Esq. of St. Andrew's Parish. (Thursday, Nov. 23, 1769.)

Last Monday died, much regretted, Whitmarsh Fuller, Esq. of St. Andrew's Parish.

Yesterday morning died, Mr. Elijah Prioleau. (Thursday, Dec. 7, 1769.)

On Tuesday died, universally regretted, John Chapman, Esq. an eminent Merchant of this Town. (Thursday, Dec. 14, 1769.)

Last Saturday Morning died, in the 71st year of her age Mrs. Judith Wragg, Relict of the Hon. Joseph Wragg, Esq.; she was a native of this Province, and as she lived universally and deservedly respected, so she died no less lamented. (Thursday Dec. 21, 1769.)

On Thursday last died, aged 84, Mrs. Ann Austin, Relict of the late Colonel Robert Austin. She arrived in this Province about 40 years of age. (Thursday, Jan. 11, 1770.)

About a month ago died at Purrysburg, aged 96 Years, Mrs. Magdalen Truan, possessing all her Faculties up to her Death; She came into this Province upwards of 30 Years ago, after having undergone the most severe Persecutions in France, during which she lived concealed for a considerable Time in the Cave of a Rock.

On Sunday last died, aged 75 Years, Mr. Daniel Bourcet, one of the oldest Inhabitants of this Town; and who, by dint of Industry, had acquired a very considerable Fortune.

Last Monday Night, died suddenly, (having been upon the Grand Jury all the Week before) James Sharp, Esq. of Ponpon; a sensible, facetious and valuable man, such as one of our most celebrated Poets stiles "the noblest Work of God." (Thursday, Jan. 25, 1770.)

Last Monday Night, died, Ebenezer Simmons, Esq. (Thursday, Feb. 1, 1770.)

Last Friday died suddenly, Captain Thomas Courtin, Master of the Brigantine Polly, of Poole, lately arrived from Newfoundland.

On Saturday last died, Mrs. Judith Guerard, the Wife of David Guerard, Esq. of St. John's Parish.

On Monday last died, John Dering, Esq. Attorney at Law. (Thursday, Feb. 15, 1770.)

Last Tuesday Night died, much regretted, and after a lingering indisposition, Thomas Gadsden, Esq. an eminent Merchant of this Town. (Thursday, March 8, 1770.)

On the 28th of last Month died, aged 77 Years, Mrs. Anne Le Bas, Relict of Mr. James Le Bas, of St. John's Parish, where she had lived forty years.

Last Monday Morning, died universally regretted, Mrs. Claudia Inglis, Wife of Mr. George Inglis, Merchant; who could not be excelled in the Characters of Christian, Wife, Mother, Friend, Mistress, &c. (Thursday, April 19, 1770.)

On Saturday last died, much regretted, Mr. Thomas Elliott, of Wappoo.

Last Tuesday night died, universally regretted, as she lived beloved; Mrs. Helena Laurens, wife of Henry Laurens, Esq. as valuable a Woman in all Respects, as any she has left behind. (Thursday, May 24, 1770.)

Yesterday died, after a very short illness, Capt. Joseph Brown, late Master of the Ship Peter & Ann, of this part. (Thursday, May 31, 1770.)

Last Sunday night died, in the 70th year of his age, universally regretted, Jacob Motte, Esq. many Years public Treasurer of this Province.

On Saturday last died, at Dorchester, Dr. James Dick. (Thursday, June 21, 1770.)

Yesterday died, universally regretted, after a lingering indisposition, and in the 71st year of his age, Isaac Mazyck, Esq. descended from an ancient and respectable family in the Isle of Rhé, that fled from the Persecutions in France. and settled in this country about the Year 1685. He was born in this Province, and always bore the most amiable character, as well in a public as a private capacity; to evince which, we need only say, that he so highly enjoyed the good opinion and confidence of the People, as to have been elected a Member in every successive Assembly of the Representatives, from the Year 1733 to this time. (Thursday, July 26, 1770.)

Last Tuesday died, after a short illness, in the 24th Year of his Age, Dr. James Dishington, whose good Sense and courteous Behaviour, rendered him greatly esteemed in Life, and equally regretted in Death. (Verses omitted).

The same Day died, Mr. John Dodd, Gunsmith. (Thursday, Aug. 9, 1770.)

Last Sunday died, aged 63 years, Mr. William Wooddrop, many

Years an eminent Merchant of this Town, who always bore a fair Character, and was much esteemed by those who knew him.

Last Sunday, died in Beaufort, ——— Holloway, Esq. Collector of His Majesty's Customs at Port-Royal. William Massey, Esq. is appointed to succeed him in that Office. (Monday Aug. 20, 1770.)

Last Sunday died, aged 66 Years (41 of which he had resided in this Province) Mr. William Carwithen, Librarian to the Charles Town Library Society. And Yesterday Mr. William Hort was elected to succeed him. (Thursday, Sept. 6, 1770.)

Last week died at the Horse-Shoe, Mr. John Law, Son to the Lieutenant Governor of the Colony of Connecticut, and lately married to the Widow of Mr. William Glover.

Last Friday Night died, aged 15 years, Miss Elizabeth Moore, a most amiable and promising young Lady, Daughter of John Moore, Esq. of St. Thomas's Parish.

Last Saturday died, at Ashepoo, aged 66 Years, Mrs. Ruth Pinckney (a Native of this Province) Widow of the late William Pinckney, Esq. Commissary General of this Province.

Last Tuesday Night died, in the 33rd Year of his age, Mr. William Williamson, who arrived here from London about four years since. He lived respected, and died regretted. (Thursday, Sept. 20, 1770.)

This Morning died, aged 45 years, Mrs. Elizabeth Lamboll, Wife of Thomas Lamboll, Esq. (Thursday, Oct. 11, 1770.)

Last Sunday Morning died, aged 53 Years, Mrs. Katharine Moody, Relict of Mr. Joseph Moody—whose Life was spent in Acts of Benevolence and Piety. (Verses omitted)

Last Monday Morning died, in the 50th Year of her Age, Mrs. Margaret Cattell, Wife of John Cattell, Esq. of St. Andrew's Parish. (Thursday, Oct. 18, 1770.)

Last Sunday died, Mr. John Lloyd Waring. (Thursday, Oct. 25, 1770.)

Last Saturday died, Mr. Johnston Rainey, Manager of Messrs. Torrans & Poaugs Distillery at Richmond, whose Conduct in Life rendered him respected, and his Death a real Loss to his Employers and Friends.

Yesterday died Mr. John Braund, Clerk and Sexton of St.

Michael's Parish; for whose place we hear, there are already several Candidates. (Thursday, Nov. 15, 1770.)

Last Saturday died, in St. Thomas's Parish aged 55 years, Mr. John Combé. (Thursday, Dec. 13, 1770.)

Last Sunday Morning died, Mrs. Mary Lowndes, the amiable Consort of the Hon. Rawlins Lowndes, Esq.; one of his Majesty's Assistant Justices and Judges of this Province—whose death is an irreparable loss to her family and friends, and universally regretted. (Thursday, Dec. 27, 1770.)

(To be continued.)

DEATH NOTICES FROM THE SOUTH CAROLINA GAZETTE FROM SEPTEMBER 29, 1766, TO DECEMBER 19, 1774

Contributed by MABEL L. WEBBER

(Continued from April)

Lately died at Savannah, Charles Watson, Esq. Clerk of his Majesty's Council; in whose Room, His Excellency Governor Wright has been pleased to appoint Alexander Wylly, Esquire. (Monday, Jan. 10, 1771)

Last Tuesday died, aged 75 years, Mr. Thomas Corker, of this Town, Merchant. (Monday, Feb. 7, 1771)

Last Sunday died, Mr. Alexander Russel, Shipwright—a very industrious honest man. (Monday, Feb. 11, 1771)

On the 6th ult. died, at his Plantation in Prince William's Parish, aged 83 years, Captain James MacPherson, a Native of this Province, who in the first Indian War, and at several other periods since, served this Country with Honour and Reputation. As he was remarkable for his Honesty, Generosity and Humanity, and more particularly for his friendly disposition, so his Death is universally regretted. (Thursday, April 4, 1771)

Last Thursday died very suddenly, William Catherwood, Esq. Barrack Master and Inspector of the outposts in Nova Scotia, and Surgeon of his Majesty's 40th Regiment at Halifax. (Thursday, May 9, 1771)

This Morning at Three o'clock died, after a very short illness, at Broom-Hall in Goose-Creek, leaving the whole Province to bewail his loss (except only those who are Enemies to the Cause of Freedom) that inestimable Member of the Community—that zealous, disinterested and unshaken Patriot—that true friend to America and the English Constitution—that excellent Man in every social relation—John Mackensie, Esq. one of the Representatives of the People of this Province in the present assembly, for the Parish of Saint James, Goose Creek. He was born in this Province the 30th day of March, 1738; received his education at the University of Cambridge, in England; lived an Honour to his Country; and,

16

we believe, no one in his sphere, ever died more universally or justly regretted. We shall forbear entering on the particulars of his character, merely because we are sensible, that we cannot do it adequate justice. By his last Will he has bequeathed the sum of Seven Thousand Pounds, towards founding, establishing and endowing a College or University in this Province; and has left his Library (which is a very valuable one) for the use of the Charles Town Library Society (tho' he was not a Member) till such University shall be established, then to be delivered up to the College.[1] (Thursday, May 30, 1771).

Last Saturday died, much regretted, Mrs. Elizabeth Smith, Wife of the Rev. Robert Smith, Rector of the Parish of St. Philip, Charles Town.

As did on Sunday, Mrs. Henrietta Stanyarne (Wife of Mr. James Stanyarne), another valuable woman. (Thursday, June 13, 1771)

Last week died, much regretted, Mrs. Elizabeth Bull, the amiable consort of Stephen Bull, Esq, of Sheldon. (Thursday, July 4, 1771)

Last Thursday night died, much lamented, Mr. Charles You, an honest man, and a facetious Companion.

On Sunday night died, after a lingering Indisposition, Mrs. Alice Weston, the Wife of Mr. Plowden Weston, Merchant.

Yesterday died, lamented by all who knew her, Mrs. Sarah Somersall, the wife of Mr. William Somersall, Merchant. (Thursday, July 18, 1771)

On the 10th instant died, Mr. Samuel Smith, Youngest Son of the late Honourable William Smith, of New York. (Thursday, Aug. 22, 1771.)

Last Sunday evening died, Mr. James Harvey, Wine Merchant. (Thursday, Sept. 5, 1771)

On Tuesday last died, Mr. James Pratt, a very honest Man, who was Door-Keeper to his Majesty's honourable Council. (Thursday, Sept. 12, 1771)

Last Monday died, much regretted by all his Acquaintance, and the Public in general, the Rev. Thomas Panting, A.M. Rector of St. Andrew's Parish, and late Master of the Free School here. (Thursday, Sept. 26, 1771)

[1] A catalogue of the library was published soon after Mackenzie's death, the Charleston Library has a copy of it.

Last Friday died at Beaufort, Port-Royal, universally regretted, the Reverend Mr. Pearce, Rector of the Parish of St. Helena—a most worthy Clergyman. (Thursday, Oct. 3, 1771)

Yesterday died, after a very short illness, Mr. John Mitchell, an eminent Deputy-Surveyor, who was reckoned as good a Judge of the Lands in this Province, as any other Person in it. (Thursday, Oct. 17, 1771)

Last night died at Stono, Mr. George Creighton, eldest son of Captain John Creighton at the Quarter-House. (Thursday, Oct. 31, 1771)

Last Thursday died, after a lingering indisposition, the amiable Mrs. Mary Huger, Wife of Benjamin Huger, Esq. (Thursday, Nov. 14, 1771.)

Last Tuesday died, Mrs. Mary Bull, a Native of this Province, aged 72 years. She was the Relict of John Bull, Esq. who was brother to the Late and Uncle to the Present Lieutenant Governor. (Thursday, Nov. 28, 1771)

Last Friday died Mrs. Mary Beale, the Wife of John Beale, Esq. much regretted by all her Friends and Acquaintance. (Thursday, Dec. 5, 1771)

Last Tuesday died, in the 71st year of his Age, (near 50 of which he practiced Physic, Surgery and Midwifery in this Province with great Reputation) that eminent, pious and truly good man, Dr. John Moultrie, so valuable a member of this community that no one who knew him can fail to lament the loss, unless destitute of the common feelings of humanity. In private and public life, in Society as well as in his Profession, he was an Example worthy of imitation.

On Tuesday last died, in the 32nd Year of her Age, after a lingering and painful Indisposition, which she bore with uncommon Fortitude and resignation, Mrs. Susannah Bee, the wife of Thomas Bee, Esq., a Lady endowed with so many excellent qualifications, that her Death is an irreparable Loss to her Family and Friends, and cannot but be lamented by everyone who had the pleasure of an Acquaintance with her.

(Dec. 1771)

Last Saturday Morning the Body of Capt. Collin McAlpine, drowned on the 15th past, floated up in the Dock near where the ship he commanded lay when he was missed. Some Gold and Silver Coin were found in one of his Breeches pockets, and his Watch in the Fob. (Tuesday, Jan. 21, 1772)

On the 14th Instant died, Mrs. Rebecca Brisbane, the Wife of James Brisbane, Esq.

Last Friday night died, John Hughes, Esq. Collector of his Majesty's Customs for this Port—"a Gentleman of such distinguished Merit, that (a Correspondent observed) it would have been impossible, had he been a Native of North Britain, to have escaped the observation of the Publisher of the General Gazette, who, in that Case, instead of barely mentioning his decease, would probably have thought he could not have said too much, or been too elaborate, for, there could not be a better Character than Mr. Hughes in private Life; no officer of the Revenue did ever give more general Satisfaction; nor has any, of so short a Residence amongst us, died more regretted. His Remains were interred the Sunday following, attended by all the principal inhabitants, next to those of his excellent Predecessor Mr. Beaufain.

Last Thursday died Mr. J. Brown, Warden of the Work house.

Last Sunday Morning died, William Roper, Esquire.

Last Saturday died Mrs. Helen Fitch, the wife of Mr. James Fitch.

On Saturday last died, Mrs. Mary Middleton, Wife of the Hon. Henry Middleton, Daughter to the late, and Sister of his Honour the present Lieutenant-Governor of this Province—a most accomplished and amiable Lady. (Thursday, March 26, 1772)

Yesterday evening died, much regretted, Mr. Isaac Lesesne, of Daniel's Island. (Thursday, March 26, 1772)

Yesterday Morning died, in the 72nd Year of his Age, Robert Quash, Esq. of St. Thomas' & St. Dennis Parish. (Thursday, April 2, 1772)

On Tuesday last died, at his Plantation on John's Island, Mr. Joseph Stanyarne, aged 72 Years, and a Native of this Province, A Gentleman so well known and respected, that whatever could be here said to preserve his Memory is needless.

The same day also died, Mrs. Judith Fraser, Widow, also a Native of this Province, aged 74 Years. (Thursday, April 9, 1772)

Last Thursday died, aged 83 Years, Mrs. Martha Combé, who had resided 68 Years in this Province.

Yesterday died, the Rev. Caleb Evans, Minister of the Congregation here, who stile themselves General Baptists. (Thursday, April 23, 1772)

On Thursday last died, much regretted, and in the 59th Year of his Age, Benjamin Simons, Esq; sometime since Commissary-General of this Province.

The same day died, Capt. John Moore, master of the ship Molly, from Liverpoole, lately arrived from the Coast of Africa. (Thursday, May 14, 1772)

Last Saturday died, Mr. Richard Rose, Son of Francis Rose, Esq. of St. Andrew's Parish.

On Tuesday died, Mr. Andrew Rutledge, Merchant of this Town. (Thursday, May 21, 1772)

This Morning died, after a few Hours illness, the Son and Heir of Sir Edmund Head. (Thursday, May 28, 1772)

On Saturday Morning died suddenly, Mr. Benjamin Roberts.

On Monday last died, after a very short illness, and very much regretted, having, by his obliging Conduct in the several spheres wherein he acted, gained universal Esteem, Mr. John Stevens, Secretary to His Majesty's Deputy-Post master General for the Southern District of North America, and Deputy Post-Master of this Town, ever since Mr. Timothy's resignation, lately elected Organist of St. Michael's Church, and also lately appointed by the Hon. George Saxby, Esq. His Majesty's Receiver General, to be his Deputy.

This Afternoon died suddenly, after having been at the Muster, Mr. James Hinds, Son of Patrick Hinds. (Thursday, June 4, 1772)

Last Sunday died, Mrs. Elizabeth Prosser, the wife of Mr. Stephen Prosser. (Thursday, June 11, 1772)

This day died, Mr. Peter Mazyck. (Thursday, June 25, 1772)

Last Friday died, much lamented, the much respected Miss Harriet Beresford, eldest daughter of Richard Beresford, Esq. Her Death was occasioned by a Consumption, a Disorder hardly known in this Province Thirty Years ago, but now so common, that three Persons were buried here last Friday and Saturday who died of it. (Thursday, July 2, 1772)

On Monday last died, of a Consumption, much lamented, Mrs. Elizabeth Martin, Wife of Mr. Sheriff Martin. (Thursday, July 16, 1772)

Died: At Black-Mingo, Mr. James Fowler, of this Town.

At. Goose-Creek, Mr. Henry Gray, sen.

At the Indian Land, Mr. William Ball, late of this Town.

In this town, Mr. Joseph Scott, son of the late Mr. Joseph Scott, of Daniel's Island.

Miss Sukey Bonette.

Miss McCormick, daughter of Alexander McCormick. (Tuesday, Aug. 25, 1772.)

Last Friday died, at his Plantation at Stono, much regretted by everyone that knew him, Archibald Stanyarne, Esq. (Monday, June 28, 1773)

This day died suddenly, the Rev. Mr. Schwab, Rector of St. Andrew's Parish, very much regretted by all his Parishoners.

A few days since also died at James-Island, Mr. La Roux, a Swiss Gentleman, who came to this Province about a twelve month ago, in Order to settle here. (Monday, July 5, 1773)

Lately died at St. Eustatius, Capt. William Rogers, formerly of this Town—And at St. Christopher's, Mr. De Port, Deputy Collector of the Customs here. (Monday, July 12, 1773)

Last Saturday evening died, Mrs. Martha Sommers, the wife of Captain John Sommers, lately gone to England.

Last night died, Mrs. Sabina Ellis, Widow of Mr. William Ellis, who died about Seven Months since, and one of whose Sons, aged 14 Years, died last Week. (Monday, July 19, 1773)

Last Thursday morning died suddenly, Mrs. Fley, Wife of Mr. Samuel Fley. (Monday, July 26, 1773).

Last Monday died, in the 86th year of her age, Mrs. Katherine Joor, who was born in Holland, and came to this Province in the year 1714. She retained all her Faculties until a little while before her Decease, and as she lived respected, so she died lamented, notwithstanding her great Age.

This Day died Mr. James Wilson, Wine Merchant, formerly in the C-partnership with Mr. John Coram. (Wednesday; Sept. 15, 1773.)

Lately died, in Prince Frederick's Parish, where he resided, Mr. Theodore Gourdin, about Forty Years of Age—He was an Honest, just Man; a good Christian, kind, benevolent, and sincere. Nothing can speak more the Praises due to his Memory, than the great number of Inhabitants attending at his House from his Death to his Interment, lamenting with Tears and bewailing their Loss, as a fond Mother would the Loss of her darling Child. In him the Poor have lost a generous Benefactor; the Rich, a Friend and Patron, the Parish, a useful Member. (Monday, Sept. 20, 1773)

Last Monday Morning died, on board the Henry Transport, Lieut. Gilbert Carter, of his Majesy's 29th Regiment.

The same Day died, Near Winyah, George Logan, Esq.

Also the same Day, Mr. Alexander McCormick, Taylor. (Monday, Sept. 27th, 1773)

Joseph Prine, one of the most notorious Villains and Horse-Thieves in America, who, though no more than 20 Years of Age, is supposed to have escaped the Gallows more than an hundred Times, last Tuesday died of a fever, in our jail, to which he had been committed but a few days before.

On Wednesday last died, (in Consequence to the Bruises he received on the 20th past, in taking a fugitive Slave belonging to his Employer) one Jacob Hans Zimmerly, Overseer to Mr. John Champneys. The Negro has since been tried, and sentenced to be executed on the 15th instant (Monday, Oct. 4, 1773)

Last Thursday Morning died, Capt. Hugh Rose, late Master of the Ship Queen Charlotte, of London.

On Saturday last died, Mrs. Barbara Creighton, Wife of Capt. John Creighton, at the Quarter House. (Monday, Oct. 11, 1773)

On Thursday last died, the ingenious Mr. William-Rigby Naylor, Architect and Surveyor. (Monday, Oct. 18, 1773)

Last Monday died, to the great Grief of the Family, and its numerous connections, Master Charles Elliott, a very promising Youth, and only Son of Charles Elliott, Esquire.

The same Day died, at Georgetown, and was brought from thence and interred here on Wednesday last, Mrs. Elizabeth Pickrow, aged 77 Years, who was a native of Philadelphia, arrived here at the Age of Five Years; and through the course of her Life delighted in Services to the Sick.

On the 8th instant died, at Black-Mingo, where he had just settled a Store, Mr. Joshua Hirst, a young Gentleman of so many good Qualities, that every one who knew, respected him, and now laments his Death.

Last Wednesday died here, much regretted by his Friends, Capt. Isaac Fordyce, late Master of the Schooner, Tobacco Packet.

A Letter from St. Augustine, dated the 11th instant, mentions the Death of Lieut. Mattier and Ensign Hallwood, both of His Majesty's 14th Regiment, and much regretted; the former on the 11th, and the latter on the 22nd of last Month, of a malignant Fever, which had made great Havock there.

Yesterday died, Mr. Charles Strother. (Monday, Oct. 25, 1773)

(To be continued)

DEATH NOTICES FROM THE SOUTH CAROLINA GAZETTE FROM SEPTEMBER 29, 1766, TO DECEMBER 19, 1774

Contributed by MABEL L. WEBBER

(Continued from July)

Died, Oct. 20th, in the Bloom of Life at James-Island, after a tedious illness, Mrs. Mary Wilson, a Lady who, to all the natural Advantages of Person, had joined those Virtues of Mind, that entitled her to the warmest affection and Esteem of her Husband and Friends whilst living, and will cause them long to regret her loss.

Since our last died, Mr. John Drayton, youngest Son of the late Thomas Drayton, Esq. (Monday, Nov. 1, 1773)

Last Tuesday died, in the Prime of Life, Mr. John Rantowle, Taylor—a literate, sensible, honest and industrious man, and a valuable member of the community. He may well be said to have lived respected, and died lamented, when his Corpse was attended to the Grave the next day, by a greater number of People of all Ranks, than are generally seen at the interment of Persons of the greatest Fortune and highest Distinction, and there were far more wet eyes. The Artillery Company, who respectfully attended his Funeral, has sustained a particular Loss in his Death; and the Society of Free and accepted Masons no less regret it,—indeed who, that knew him, does not?

On Thursday last died, in St. Andrew's Parish, the ingenious Mr Thomas Mellichamp, who some Years ago discovered an entire new Method of producing Flora Indico. (Monday, Nov. 8, 1773)

On Tuesday, died at Stono, exceedingly regretted by his Parishoners and all who knew him, the Rev. John Tonge, Rector of St. Paul's Parish.

Last Saturday died, after a short Illness, Mr. Dandridge Clifford, a most promising Youth, and only Son of the late Mr. John Clifford.

Yesterday died, Mrs. Ann Simmons, the amiable Consort of

24

James Simmons, Esq. who lately also lost one of his Children, and is extremely ill himself. (Monday, Nov. 22, 1773)

There have died within a Month past, in the Parishes of St. Stephen and St. James, Santee, the following Persons, in advanced Ages, viz:

In the 82nd Year of her Age, 74 of which she had lived in this Province, Mrs. Mary Stewart, a Native of the Island of St. Helena, who could see and do coarse work, and thread a Needle without Spectacles, within a fortnight of her Death.

In the 76th Year of his Age, Mr. William Johnson, a Native of Ireland, and 66 Years an Inhabitant of this Province.

In the 73rd Year of his Age, Mr. Francis DesChamps, born in Paris, an Inhabitant of the Parish he died in near 50 Years.

In the 105th Year of his Age, Mr. James Jaquette, a Native of Switzerland, near 60 years a Resident at Santee. He was one of a Party of Deserters, who compelled the Master of a French Transport-Ship from Mobille, to bring them to this Port, and two of his Comrades are still living. (Monday, Nov. 29, 1773)

On Tuesday died, Mr. Alexander Peronneau, junior, son of Alexander Peronneau, Esq.

Yesterday died, much lamented by all who knew her, Mrs. Charlotte McCall, the wife of Mr. John McCall, jun. (Monday, Dec. 6, 1773)

Last Tuesday died, in the 72nd year of her Age, Mrs. Katharine Beale, Widow of the late Honorable Othniel Beale, and Mother to the Lady of his Honour the Lieutenant Governour.

The same day died, John Ainslie, Esq. who some time since married Lady Mary, one of the Daughters of the Earl of Cromartie.

Last Monday died very suddenly, at his Plantation in St. Paul's parish, in the full Strength and Bloom of Life, Mr. Benjamin Williamson, a young Gentleman of so excellent a Character and disposition, that none, who knew him living, can avoid regretting his Death.

The same Day died, much lamented, Mrs. Elizabeth Scott, Wife of Mr. William Scott, Merchant.

The same day died, Mrs. Martha Ferguson, Wife of Thomas Ferguson, Esq. than whom there was not a better wife, Mother, Friend, Mistress, or greater Benefactress to the Poor and Helpless; so that her Loss is not only irreparable to her Family, but also to every one who knew her, especially the Distressed.

On Wednesday also died, the Hon. John Murray, M.D. one of his Majesty's Assistant Judges for this Province—who some Years since married Lady Ann, another Daughter of the Earl of Cromartie, and Widow of the Honourable Edmond Atkin, First Superintendent of Indian Affairs for the Southern District. (Monday, Jan. 17, 1774)

"The 11th Instant, died in Child-Bed, at Beaufort, Port-Royal, Mrs. Mary Elliott, Wife of William Elliott, Esq. a Lady endowed with every Qualification that could dignify human nature." (Monday, Jan. 24, 1774)

On Monday last died, very suddenly, Mr. Samuel Cardy, the ingenious Architest, who undertook and completed the building of St. Michael's Church in this Town, and the Beacon or Light-House on Middle-Island, near the Bar. (Monday, Jan. 31, 1774)

On Thursday last died, Mrs. Jane Remington, the wife of Mr. John Remington, jun. (Monday, Feb. 14, 1774)

The same Day the Body of Capt. Terence McDonough, the Commander of the Comet Packet Boat, who was unfortunately drowned on the 5th ult., floated into the Market Dock, near the Place where he fell into the River, and the same evening was decently interred.

The same Day died, Mrs. Ann Bell, Widow of Colonel Thomas Bell, and Sister to the late Mr. Justice Murray. (Monday, Feb. 21, 1774)

On Saturday last died, Mr. William Cripps, Taylor. (Monday, Feb. 28, 1774)

On Tuesday last died, John Cattell, Esq; (Son of William) of St. Andrew's Parish.

This morning died, Mr. Fortescue, one of the Lieutenants of His Majesty's Ship Glasgow. (Monday, March 21, 1774)

This morning died, much regretted by all that knew her, the amiable Mrs. Sarah Matthewes, Wife of John Matthewes, Esq. Son of James. (Monday, March 28, 1774)

Last Thursday night died, Mr. Algernon Wilson, of St. Paul's Parish. (Monday, April 4, 1774)

On Wednesday last died, the Rev. William Davies, Rector of St. Mark's Parish in this Province.

On the 9th past, died at New York, Capt. Thomas Sowers, principal Engineer in America. General Haldemand has appointed

Captain John Montresor to succeed the Deceased. (Monday, April 11. 1774)

Lately died in North Carolina, the Honourable Samuel Swann, one of the first settlers on Cape Fear River, aged 70 years. He had been Speaker of several Houses of Representatives there 19 Years. (Monday, April 18, 1774)

Last Friday Morning died, Alexander Peronneau, Esq. in the— year of his Age. (Monday, April 25, 1774)

Last Thursday died, Capt. William Hayman, Master of the Ship Bacchus, of Liverpoole, lately arrived from Africa. (Monday, May 16, 1774)

On Wednesday last died, a very ingenious and honest man, Mr. Jeremiah Theus, who had followed the business of a Portrait-painter here upwards of thirty years.

Last Friday died, much lamented, Mrs. Elizabeth Smith, Relict of the late Thomas Smith, sen. Esq. a Lady that was endowed with every good Qualification, besides being a most devout Christian. (Monday, May 23, 1774)

Last Tuesday night died, of an Apoplectic fit, Mrs. Rebecca Rutledge, the Wife of Mr. Andrew Rutledge.

Last Thursday died, Miss Polly Ford, a very amiable young lady, daughter of the late Mr. Ford, of Ponpon.

Last Friday died, Mr. William Foord. (Monday, May 30, 1774)

Yesterday morning died, universally lamented, Mr. Knight Giball—a most worthy Gentleman. (Monday, June 6, 1774)

On Tuesday last died. Mr. Paul Villepontoux, Gunner of Fort Johnson. (Monday, June 20, 1774)

Since our last died, Mrs. Sarah Edmonds.—Mrs. Bush, wife of Mr. John Bush, Merchant, and Mr. Jacob Axson, sen, for some years past one of the Messengers of the Commons House of Assembly of this Province. (Monday, June 27, 1774)

Death. The Reverend John Martin, A.M. Minister at Willtown. "He was an animated evengelic preacher. His abilities, natural and acquired, were very great, and all devoted to the Service of God and his Country. What he preached in the Pulpit, his Life preached out of it; the Tenor of his Behaviour being, as it were, a practical comment on that poor Religion he warmly recommended to others. In his Life, there was not a good Action scattered here and there, but, like the Milky Way, it was thick set with the genuine Fruits of sincere Piety and active Benevolence. The Doctrines of Grace he firmly believed and invariably preached, and on them resting his Soul's salvation, he welcomed Death with such a Heavenborn Tranquillity, as would have extorted a wish from the Sons of Vice and Folly. That they might die the Death of the Righteous, and their last End be like his." (Monday, July 4, 1774)

Some time about last Thursday night died, much regretted, Mrs. Frances Spence, the amiable Consort of Doctor Peter Spence, of Ponpon, and Daughter of Joseph Brown, Esq. of Georgetown. (Monday, July 11, 1774)

Last Thursday died, Mr. John Parnham, formerly a merchant in this Town.

Last Wednesday died, Mrs. Sarah Tucker, Wife of Capt. Thomas Tucker; a valuable woman.

On Saturday last died, much regretted, Mr. Oliver Dale, Schoolmaster; some of whose Pupils had, no longer than the Thursday se'nnight before, presented the Tragedy of Cato, with Applause, at the Theatre in this Town.

The same Day died, at Ashley-Ferry, much regretted by his Congregation, the Rev. Philip Dobell, a Preacher of the Society who distinguish themselves by the Name of General Baptists.

This Day died, Mr. Richard Gill, Master of his Majesty's Ship Glasgow—a good old Officer.

On Thursday last died, at Ashley-Ferry, the Rev. Daniel Dobell, a General Baptist Preacher, Son of the Rev. Philip Dobell, who died at the same Place on the 20th Instant.

Mr. Charles Boyd, one of the unfortunate Persons, who was blown up in firing the Salute at the Market-Wharf on Sunday the 14 ult, died last Tuesday. -He has left a poor Widow and Daughter. (Monday, Sept. 19, 1774)

Last Tuesday Morning died, a most humane and generous spirited young Gentleman—Mr. Michael Meara, Nephew to James Parsons, Esq.

Last Night died, much regretted, Mr. Aaron Simonson, a young Gentleman who a few Years since came into this Province from New York, with Mr. Jeremiah Brower, with whom he established himself in the commercial way here. (Monday, Sept. 26, 1774)

Yesterday morning died, Mr. James Guerin, a very promising

young Man, Son of Mr. Mathurin Guerin, of St. Andrew's Parish. (Monday, Oct. 3, 1774)

Last Saturday died, much regretted, Mr. Arthur Peronneau, Brother to Mr. Treasurer Peronneau. (Monday, Oct. 17, 1774)

Thursday evening, died suddenly, at His House in George-Yard, Lombard-Street, London, Mr. Richard Grubb, a Carolina Merchant. (Monday, Oct. 24, 1774)

Last Friday died, much regretted by the whole Parish, to which, as well as to his Family and Friends his Death is an irreparable Loss, Daniel Ravenell, sen, Esq. of St. John's Parish, in Berkeley County.

Yesterday died, Miss Sarah Croft, the last of the Family of the late Childemas Croft, Esq.

Last Saturday evening died, in the 81st, or as some suppose, in the 85th year of his age, Thomas Lamboll, Esq; a gentleman of proverbial Integrity and Uprightness, and much lamented, tho' he died at so late a Period. He had sustained sundry honourable Employments in the Government with great Dignity, but for a long time past had declined public Business, contented to serve Mankind in a Sphere where he might be useful tho' less conspicuous. Perhaps all the papers now in the Province do not contain so good an History of it as was recorded in his Memory. He has not left a Person so well acquainted with all its concerns as himself. He was an honest and truly religious Man, without Affectation. He lived usefully, and he died comfortably. In steady reliance upon the only Hope of a Christian, he entered the Valley of Death as he used to enter his Office. He well understood what he was about, in an Hour which comes upon others with surprise, and is one of those few Instances, in which a Man, dying above Fourscore, is greatly missed and sincerely lamented. (Monday, Oct. 31, 1774)

Last Saturday died, aged 71, Mr. Solomon Legare, a native of this Province, and as good a Man as ever lived or died. Neither Scarves, gloves or Mourning were used at this Funeral, altho' he left a very numerous Train of most affection relations; who have thereby conformed to the 8th Article of the Association entered into by the late Congress, in Behalf and on the part of the Colonies. (Monday, Nov. 21, 1774)

On Sunday the 4th instant, died, after a lingering indisposition, and exceedingly regretted by her numerous relations and friends, Mrs. Rebecca Webb, the Wife of Benjamin Webb, Esq.

Last Tuesday died here, a worthy good Woman, Mrs. Katharine Poinsett, Widow of Mr. Elisha Poinsett. (Dec. 12, 1774)

The Remains of Mrs. Mary Elliott (the Wife of the Hon. Barnard Elliott) who died in Child-bed, on Sunday the 11th Instant, were interred on Wednesday last. Few have left more Relations, few had more Friends, than this most amiable and excellent Lady, yet the latter clause of the 8th article of the Continental Association was strictly adhered to at this funeral.

On Friday the 9th Instant, died at Hobcaw, in the 72nd Year of his Age, Mr. David Linn, who was much esteemed by all his Acquaintances, and has left a considerable Fortune to be enjoyed by some poor relations. (Monday, Dec. 19, 1774)

INDEX